HOW JOHNNY POPPER REPLACED THE HORSE

A HISTORY OF JOHN DEERE TWO-CYLINDER TRACTORS
PUBLISHED BY DEERE & COMPANY/MOLINE, ILLINOIS

CONTENTS

© 1988 by Deere & Company, John Deere Road, Moline, Illinois 61265. International Standard Book Number: ISBN 0-86691-111-1. Library of Congress Catalogue Card Number: 87-73444.

DEDICATION

This book is dedicated to the thousands of members worldwide of the Two-Cylinder Club who are keeping alive a portion of early American farm history; and to the hundreds of members who generously made available their restored tractors and equipment to be photographed for this and future books.

Page 2: This Model "AI" Tractor was photographed in 1936 pulling a freight car at the John Deere Waterloo, Iowa, factory. The "AI" was an industrial version of the popular Model "A" farm tractor.

Right: Restoring antique tractors is a great father-son, wintertime project. Needed parts can be salvaged from unrestorable tractors or built from scratch. Many old parts and service manuals are still available. The simplicity of the early John Deere 2-cylinder tractors makes them easy to repair and restore. Compared to modern tractors, these antiques have very few moving parts.

Early model antique tractors are difficult to find today because many patriotic farmers donated old tractors to scrap metal drives during World War II. But a few can still be found in abandoned barns, junkyards and used farm equipment lots. Some North American collectors have even gone to Europe and South America in search of specific models.

INTRODUCTION

The John Deere tractors produced between 1918 and 1960 occupy a special niche in the history of farm mechanization. Their unique horizontal 2-cylinder engine design sets them apart from tractors manufactured by most of the other companies. Another unique characteristic was the low engine speed—as slow as 750 revolutions per minute. These early John Deere tractors were renowned not only for their lugging power, dependability, simplicity and outstanding fuel economy, but also for their distinctive sound.

Some farmers characterized the engine exhaust noise as a "putt-putt," others said it was more like a "pop-pop." Either way, farmers could easily distinguish a "two lunger" John Deere from any other tractor, even when the tractors couldn't be seen.

In many rural, Midwestern communities, these early 2-cylinder John Deeres were affectionately referred to as "Poppin' Johnnies," because of their unique sound. In other communities, they were commonly called "Johnny Poppers."

Like most early mechanical devices, the 2-cylinder John Deere tractors evolved during their 40-year life span from a rather crude contraption to a highly refined, well-tuned piece of modern machinery. As each model was introduced, it was thought at the time to be strictly "state of the art." But each model was improved by John Deere engineers and was followed by a more innovative offering with more power, more productivity, more comfort or more convenience, or often all of these benefits rolled into one shiny new tractor.

By the 1950s, these tractors had hundreds of thousands of rural devotees. In fact, many farmers were convinced that Deere & Company had made a serious error in judgment when it announced in 1960 that the basic 2-cylinder engine would be discontinued, and that John Deere was joining the rest of the farm equipment industry with a line of 4- and 6-cylinder tractors. These loyal enthusiasts forgot, or chose to overlook, the fact that the early 2-cylinder tractors were originally developed simply as a replacement for the horse. In their day, these 2-cylinder tractors were right for the times, but the times had changed and they were no longer right for the future.

Promotional literature for the early 2-cylinder tractors proudly claimed that "everything that can be done on the farm by horses or by a heavy-duty stationary or portable engine, can be accomplished by a Waterloo Boy"—John Deere's first 2-cylinder tractor. That was in the 1910s. Thirty years later, the 2-cylinder Model "LA" Tractor was introduced and cited as being "powered to pull all loads ordinarily handled with a 3-horse team..." Even into the mid-1940s with the introduction of the new 2-cylinder Model "M" Tractors, product literature reminded farmers that "...many horse-drawn implements can be adapted to use with the Model 'M'..."

Yes, Johnny Popper replaced the horse, and in doing so created a following of loyal enthusiasts. Hundreds of 2-cylinder John Deere tractors have been rescued from rural junkyards, weed patches or from behind bales of hay in the corner of some barn and painstakingly restored. On the following pages are photographs of many of the original tractors and several of these mint-condition, restored models. Also included is information on the various tractor models, the sequence of introduction and their significant mechanical features.

This book was written for those people who have an interest in old farm and industrial tractors, specifically antique 2-cylinder John Deere tractors. Admittedly, many details and facts about model variations of different tractors have been omitted.

WATERLOO BOY

The Waterloo Boy Tractor was advertised as "The Original Kerosene Tractor." It also was the "original" John Deere 2-cylinder tractor even though it never carried the John Deere brand name.

Deere & Company bought the Waterloo Gasoline Engine Company of Waterloo, Iowa, in 1918, after several years of experimenting on its own with various tractor designs. The Waterloo Gasoline Engine Company was formed by John Froelich shortly after he developed in 1892 the first gasoline-engine-powered farm tractor that could be driven both forward and in reverse.

The first Waterloo Boy Tractor was sold in 1914; it was the Model "L." The Model "R" replaced the "L" and was introduced in 1915 and built through 1919. The Model "N" was built and sold from 1917 through 1924. The models "L" and "R" had only one forward speed while the Model "N" had two forward speeds: 2¼ and 3 miles per hour. The reverse speed was 1¾ miles per hour.

The Model "N" was known as a 12-25 tractor, delivering 12 horsepower at the drawbar and 25 horsepower at the belt pulley at 750 revolutions per minute. The "N" also was called a "3-plow tractor," because it could pull three 14-inch plow bottoms through normal soil conditions; or a 9-foot double-action disk harrow; or two binders through heavy grain. It had ample belt power to operate a stationary corn sheller, hay baler, ensilage cutter or grain separator.

The Waterloo Boy Tractors had several interesting mechanical features. For instance, the transmission was located on the left side of the engine, instead of in-line or behind the engine. It had automotive-type sliding gears that were in mesh only when the tractor was traveling, not when it was doing belt work. The belt pulley was driven directly off the crankshaft. A combination forced-feed and splash lubrication system kept all engine and transmission bearing points and gears constantly in an oil bath.

The Waterloo Boy had a water-cooled, horizontal 2-cylinder engine that burned kerosene, a heavier petroleum distillate than gasoline. When the engine was running, heat from the exhaust manifold vaporized the kerosene as it entered the cylinders, resulting in excellent combustion. The result was more work with less fuel—a cost savings farmers clearly appreciated. Water cooled the engine and was circulated by a centrifugal pump through a large honeycomb-type radiator. Both the radiator fan and the water pump were driven by V-belts directly from the flywheel.

Initially, the Waterloo Boy Tractors had a drum-and-chain steering system. In 1920, a rod-type, automotive-type steering system became available.

Although there were only three basic Waterloo Boy models—the "L," "R" and "N"—there were several different versions built. The "R" Tractors usually can be identified by the radiator, which was mounted on the right side behind a small-diameter, horizontal fuel tank. Also, the spur gear attached to each rear wheel is of a smaller diameter than the rear wheel.

The "N" Tractors have a radiator mounted on the left side behind a large-diameter fuel tank; and the spur gear is nearly the same diameter as the rear wheel. Some "Rs" have a round vertical fuel tank.

Although most Waterloo Boy Tractors were sold and used on farms in North America, many were exported. In Great Britain they were sold as the Overtime Tractor. In that country, they burned "paraffin," the British name for kerosene.

Though crude in design by modern standards, the Waterloo Boy Tractors helped to establish the reputation that John Deere 2-cylinder tractors enjoyed for nearly 40 years for economy, simplicity, dependability and long life.

Here's an early model Waterloo Boy Tractor. This photograph was taken in 1918. Note the spring-cushioned, chain-link steering and the side placement of the tractor seat. Sitting sideways was thought to be an advantage, enabling the operator to look forward for steering and backward at the work being done with equal ease.

WATERLOO BOY TRACTOR

BURNS KEROSENE COMPLETELY

JOHN DEERE
MOLINE, ILL.

Points of Merit

1. **Simple Design**—easy to understand—you can expert it yourself.
2. **Burns Kerosene.** Patented manifold gasifies the kerosene and saves many dollars in fuel cost every year. No kerosene to work past piston rings into crank case to destroy quality of lubricating oil and result in burning out bearings.
3. **Powerful Two-Cylinder Engine** delivers its full rated 25 horse-power on belt and 12 horse-power on draw-bar.
4. **Heavy Two-Throw Balanced Crank Shaft** —long-lived motor and increased power due to lack of vibration.
5. **Simple and Positive Oiling System** —automatic—extremely low oil consumption.
6. **Water Cooled** by large core radiator. Capacity of cooling system, 13 gallons. Water circulated by reliable centrifugal pump.
7. **Reliable Ignition**—simple high tension magneto with impulse starter.
8. **Extra Strong Gears,** case-hardened, heat-treated, dust-proof, run in oil.
9. **Roller Bearings** at all important points reduce friction and conserve power.
10. **Right-Hand Drive Wheel in Furrow**—a big advantage in plowing—prevents side draft on plow and tractor. Self-steering.
11. **Pulley Driven Direct** from engine crank shaft—a big advantage in belt work—no gears in mesh—every ounce of power utilized.
12. **Low Repair Cost** and John Deere repair service.

KEROSENE

WATERLOO BOY

Pulling a John Deere 3-bottom plow. Drive wheel in furrow—no plow or tractor side draft.

Pulling John Deere Heavy Tractor Disc Harrow and Brillion Pulverizer—good seed beds rapidly.

Pulling two John Deere 8-foot binders—gets the harvesting done at the right time.

Furnishing belt power for a John Deere Corn Sheller —no gears in mesh at belt work.

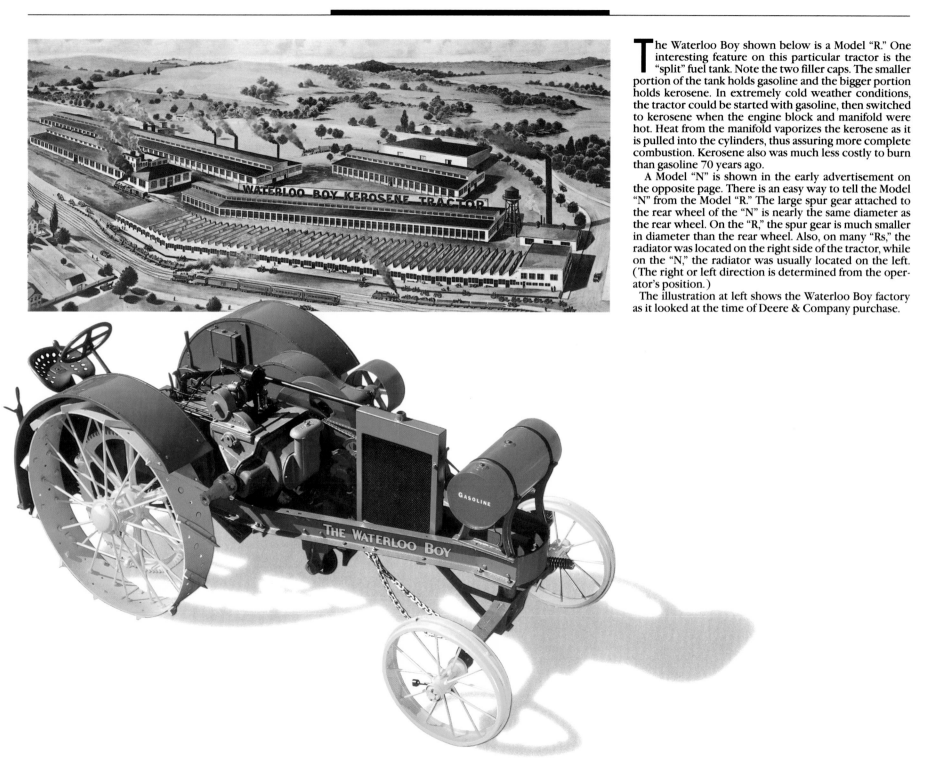

The Waterloo Boy shown below is a Model "R." One interesting feature on this particular tractor is the "split" fuel tank. Note the two filler caps. The smaller portion of the tank holds gasoline and the bigger portion holds kerosene. In extremely cold weather conditions, the tractor could be started with gasoline, then switched to kerosene when the engine block and manifold were hot. Heat from the manifold vaporizes the kerosene as it is pulled into the cylinders, thus assuring more complete combustion. Kerosene also was much less costly to burn than gasoline 70 years ago.

A Model "N" is shown in the early advertisement on the opposite page. There is an easy way to tell the Model "N" from the Model "R." The large spur gear attached to the rear wheel of the "N" is nearly the same diameter as the rear wheel. On the "R," the spur gear is much smaller in diameter than the rear wheel. Also, on many "Rs," the radiator was located on the right side of the tractor, while on the "N," the radiator was usually located on the left. (The right or left direction is determined from the operator's position.)

The illustration at left shows the Waterloo Boy factory as it looked at the time of Deere & Company purchase.

The Model "N" Waterloo Boy Tractor shown at right was among the last ones built in 1924. Note that steel rods have replaced the chain-link steering used on earlier models. When the State of Nebraska initiated its farm tractor testing program, a Model "N" Waterloo Boy was the first tractor tested. That was in 1920. The "N" was certified as having 12 horsepower at the drawbar and 25 horsepower at the belt pulley with the kerosene-burning engine operating at 750 revolutions per minute. At right is one of the small oil tanks mounted on top of each rear fender. An oil line connected to this tank was located so oil could be dripped on the final-drive and spur gear attached to the rear wheels. By opening a small petcock, the operator could lubricate each final drive while the tractor was in motion.

At far right is a photograph of the steering mechanism on the front axle of the late Model "N" Tractor. A steering rod turned a worm gear which moved the half-moon shaped gear that turned the front wheels. Simplicity and easy access for service was one of the big advantages of owning an early John Deere tractor. The photograph on the next page was taken on the Waterloo Boy Tractor assembly line about 1923. Note that the belt pulley has not been attached.

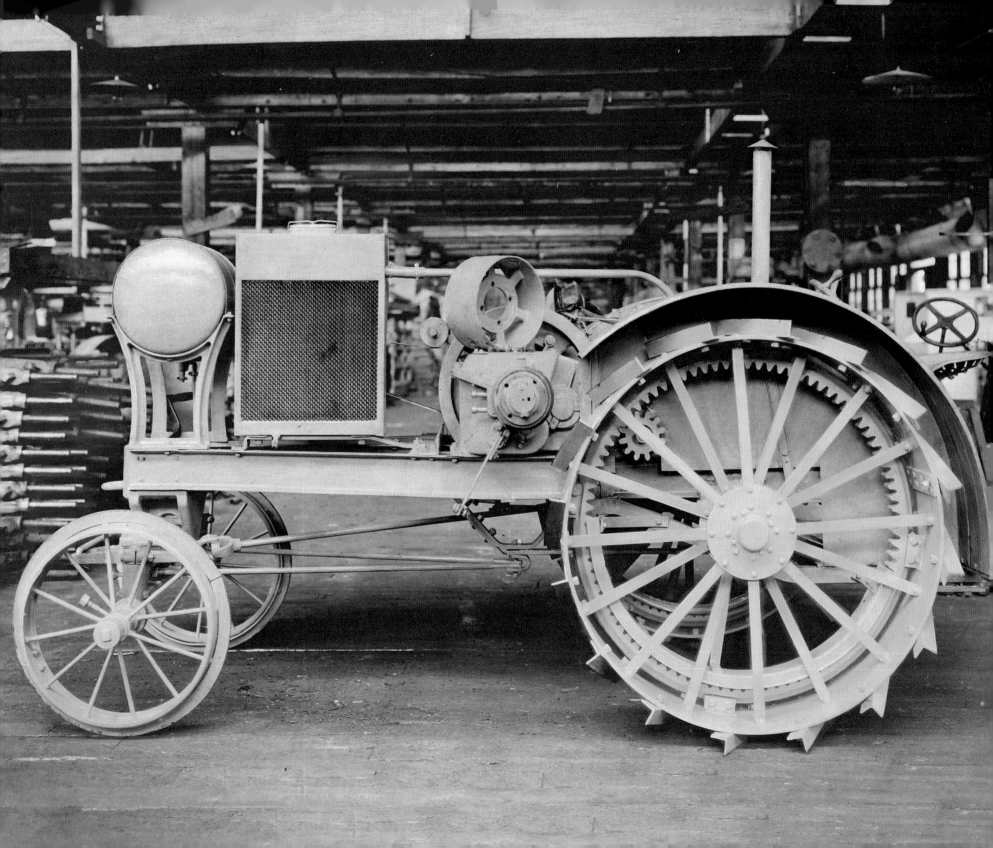

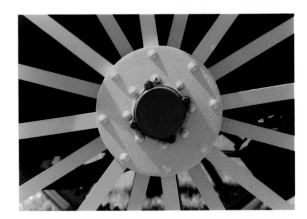

Shown at right is an old showroom poster for the Waterloo Boy. This was distributed to dealers around 1916 and predated the purchase of the Waterloo Gasoline Engine Company by Deere & Company.

Above on the left is a photograph of the rear-wheel hub of a Model "R" Waterloo Boy Tractor, showing details of its construction.

The photograph on the right shows a unique mechanical design feature of the Waterloo Boy. Note that the transmission is located to the left of the engine—not "in-line" as subsequent tractors were designed. Also note that the flywheel is located between the engine and the transmission and that the crankshaft is on the right side of the engine and the belt pulley is on the left side of the transmission. The transmission case cover could be removed for complete access to transmission and differential gears and bearings. The crankcase cover also could be removed easily, giving ready access to connecting rods and crankshaft bearings.

On the opposite page a Model "N" is shown in the process of moving a large storage shed. With the horizontal, 2-cylinder engine, the Waterloo Boy and later John Deere tractors were well known for lugging power.

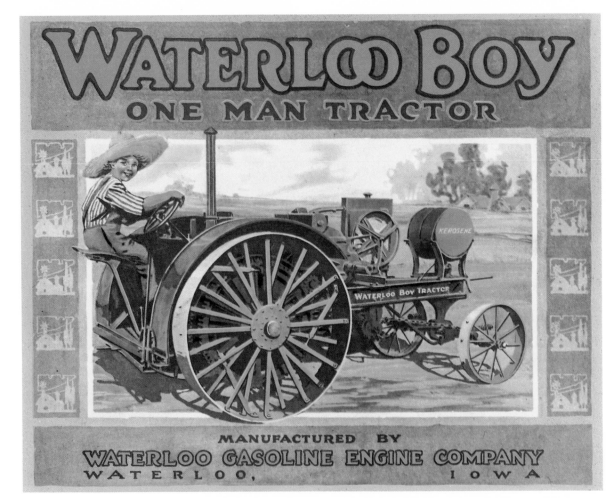

vertime was the brand name under which Waterloo Boy Tractors were sold in the United Kingdom. The tractor at right is a 1917 Model "R." It was brought back to the United States from Ireland and restored. This tractor really stands out in a display of traditionally colored John Deere Tractors, because of its red-orange wheels, dark green fenders and frame and gray engine, fuel tank and radiator.

On the opposite page, the upper left and center photographs show details of a restored, portable stationary Waterloo Boy Engine. The left photograph is of the belt pulley with friction hand clutch for engaging and disengaging. The center photograph is of the exposed valve train on a "T-type" Stationary Engine.

The upper right photograph is the brass radiator-drain petcock on a Waterloo Boy Tractor. The field scene on the opposite page was photographed in 1919. It shows a John Deere Van Brunt grain drill being pulled by a Model "R" Waterloo Boy Tractor. Note the horizontal fuel tank on this tractor and compare it to the vertical fuel tank shown in the close-up at far lower right. Early sales literature shows that a wide variety of fuel tanks, both horizontal and vertical, were used on Waterloo Boy Tractors.

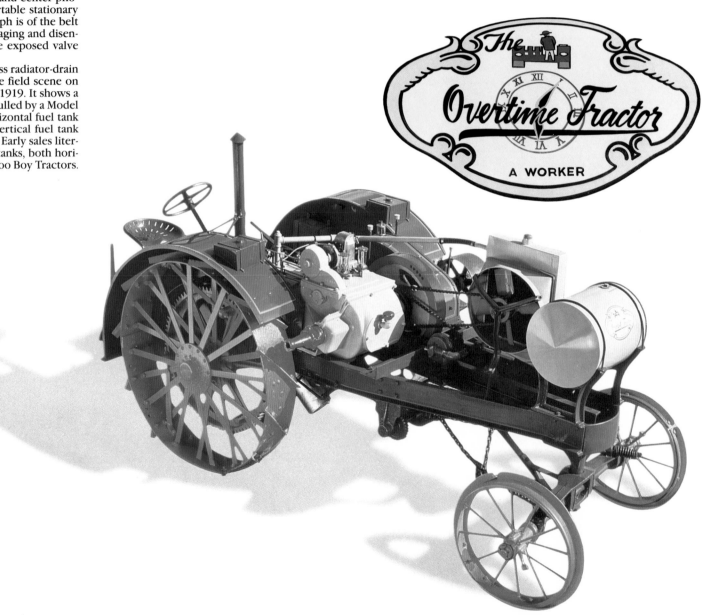

The *Overtime Tractor*
A WORKER

MODEL D

When Deere & Company purchased the Waterloo Gasoline Engine Company in 1918, one of the first priorities was to improve the current Waterloo Boy Tractors. Deere wanted to increase sales in order to gain a firm foothold in the fledgling farm tractor market. Simultaneously, however, while improvements were being made development work was started on a new tractor to replace the Waterloo Boy.

Engineers had talked with dealers and farmers and knew what improvements were needed: greater power, yet lighter weight; simpler construction and operation; more compact and maneuverable. The John Deere Model "D" introduced in 1923 met all of these criteria so well it remained in the line for 30 years—the longest of any John Deere tractor.

Although not the first tractor to bear the John Deere name, the Model "D" was the first John Deere tractor to be produced in a substantial quantity.

Barnyard folklore has it that the "D" model designation stood for dependability . . . a trait for which the "D" became world famous. Actually, the "D" model designation came about because this tractor configuration was the fourth prototype to be developed and the one selected for production.

The "D" retained many of the desirable features of the Waterloo Boy. It had a large-displacement 2-cylinder, water-cooled, horizontal engine that burned kerosene and other low-cost fuels. In fact, farmers used to joke that the "D" would burn anything flammable they could pour in the fuel tank. The engine in the "D," however, was turned 180 degrees from its position in the Waterloo Boy. The combustion chamber and spark plugs were located near the front of the tractor. The crankshaft was located near the middle of the tractor. The transmission was placed in-line and behind the engine. Both the belt pulley and the flywheel were mounted directly on the crankshaft, but the belt pulley was on the opposite side from where it was located on the Waterloo Boy.

The original "D" was rated at Nebraska with 27 horsepower at the belt pulley at 800 revolutions per minute and 15 horsepower at the drawbar. That was 25 percent more drawbar power than the Model "N" Waterloo Boy. Before the "D" ended its career, it was rated with 42 horsepower at the belt at 900 revolutions per minute and 38 horsepower at the drawbar (observed horsepower). The "D" was considered a 3- or 4-plow-bottom tractor—depending on soil conditions—yet it weighed no more than three good draft horses.

Like the Waterloo Boy, the early "D" had two forward speeds (2½ and 3¼ mph) and a 2 miles per hour reverse speed. In 1936, the "D" was given three forward speeds: 2½, 3¼ and 4½ miles per hour. The reverse speed remained the same. The final drive was a double-roller chain and remained so during the 30-year life of this tractor.

Early production "Ds" had a 26-inch diameter cast-iron flywheel with six spokes. In 1925, the flywheel was reduced to 24 inches in diameter, but retained the 6-spoke design. Today, these two model "D" versions are called "spokers" by antique tractor buffs. In 1926, the spokes were eliminated and the flywheel was redesigned as a smooth, solid casting.

Operator safety, comfort and convenience were taken into consideration in the design of the "D" Tractor. It had a flat, roomy operator's platform which was easy to step on or off. It was enclosed on two sides by large, rounded fenders which extended close to the flywheel and belt pulley. The seat was adjust-

The Model "D" Tractor at left is pulling a grain binder with an operator. Long control levers became available in a few years that enabled the binder operator to run the tractor, making grain binding a one-man job. The photograph above is of a rear-wheel hub on a Model "D" Tractor.

able and attached to a sturdy support. On later versions, the seat support was attached to a spring to reduce operator fatigue.

The early "D" had the steering wheel located on the left-hand side of the operator's area. When the flywheel was reduced in size, a joint was put in the steering column and the steering wheel was moved toward the centerline. In 1931, worm-type steering was installed and the steering wheel and operator seat were placed slightly to the right of the center of the tractor.

Because the "D" was shorter in length than the Waterloo Boy, it had a tighter turning radius and was much more maneuverable. It could be turned more quickly at the end of the row and positioned more easily for belt work. Farmers appreciated these two design benefits.

Another feature farmers said they liked was that parts were simple and easy to replace. Nearly all service and repair work could be done by the farmer standing up.

Model "D" Tractors built between 1923 and 1939 are commonly referred to as "unstyled." In 1939, the "D" received a face-lift to give it an improved appearance similar to the restyled Model "A" and "B" Tractors, which were by then in the line. The "D" Tractors built after mid-1939 are referred to as "styled." A new grille with several vertical lines enclosed the radiator and a new hood with smooth horizontal lines gave the "D" a more modern appearance.

Also, by 1939, more than 50 percent of the "D" Tractor orders specified the optional rubber-tired wheels, so the deci-

The Model "D" underwent many changes in its 30-year life. Front left is a 1923 model—one of the earliest ones built. Upper left is a later Model "D." Both of these "Ds" have a spoked flywheel; collectors call such models "spoker." Next to it is a later Model "D" with a solid flywheel. Note that the three models on the opposite page all have air intakes and exhausts that extend well above their hoods. This indicates that they are 1931 or later models. The yellow tractor is a 1936 Industrial version, designated a "DI." Fewer than 100 were built. The upper right tractor on page 21 is a 1938 model. It was among the last of the unstyled models built. The "D" in the foreground was built in the 1950s. It is called a styled model.

sion was made to switch from steel wheels to rubber-tired wheels as regular equipment. However, for a few years during World War II, steel wheels became standard again, because rubber tires were difficult to obtain.

Electric starting, electric lights and a powershaft (known today as a power takeoff or PTO) were also popular options. The powershaft was available on tractors built as early as the mid-1920s. It was used to power such pull-type equipment as corn pickers and grain binders.

Different versions of the "D" were built for special applications. The orchard version had smaller diameter wheels and a "laid down" exhaust and air intake. Special fenders were available for tractors used in rice or sugarcane fields. A few "Ds" were even converted into crawlers and the "DI" with rubber tires was built for industrial or highway maintenance work.

The Model "D" established John Deere in the farm tractor business. Because it was low cost, economical to run, maneuverable, easy to operate and service, durable and dependable, the "D" became one of the most popular tractors available. It was such a popular model, in fact, that after the "D" assembly line was dismantled, 92 tractors were assembled in June and July 1953, from surplus parts in order to fill additional dealer orders. Because these tractors were built in a roadway between two Waterloo factory buildings, they were nicknamed "streeters" by the factory workers. These "streeters" can be identified by their serial numbers and are sought after today by restorers, because they represent the last build of a truly great tractor.

It took hundreds of hours of painstaking labor to restore to mint condition the Model "D" pictured on the opposite page.

At left is a front cover of a 1938 Model "D" Tractor sales folder. John Deere included many user testimonials to substantiate its "the economical tractor" claim.

In the early 1900s, many farm equipment dealerships included a nearby horse barn where horses and mules taken in on trade for a new or used tractor were stabled until resold or traded.

Shown below is a 1924 Model "D." In the early years it was frequently referred to as a "15-27" tractor, because it delivered 15 horsepower at the drawbar and 27 horsepower at the belt pulley. When the "D" was discontinued in 1953, it was observed at 38 horsepower at the drawbar and 42 horsepower at the belt. This 1924 model had a list price of $950. The unstyled "D" and the "GP" Tractor, which was introduced in 1929, were similar in appearance except for the front axles. The "D" has a straight, horizontal axle, while the "GP" front axle is arched. The "D" delivered power three ways: at the drawbar, the belt pulley and the powershaft (PTO). Shown at right is a typical belt pulley application.

Early production "Ds" had a 26-inch diameter cast-iron flywheel with six spokes, as shown at far upper right. In 1925, the flywheel was reduced to 24 inches but the spoke design was retained. In 1926, the spokes were eliminated in favor of a smooth, solid casting, as shown at far lower right.

Above is a 1930 Model "D" Tractor equipped with spoked wheels and rubber tires. Many farmers converted their tractors to rubber for the smoother ride and ease of transporting. In the late 1930s, more tractors were ordered from the factory "on rubber" than with steel wheels, so rubber-tired wheels became regular equipment. With the rubber shortage during World War II, steel wheels became regular equipment again for a few years.

At left is a photograph of the power takeoff assembly on a "D." Originally the powershaft was a dealer-installed option; later it became a factory-installed "extra."

At far left is a spark arrester attached to the exhaust pipe on a Model "D." This attachment prevented sparks from the tractor engine from igniting dry chaff in the barn or stubble in the field.

On the opposite page is a styled Model "D" Tractor as it appeared in 1941.This "look" lasted throughout the remainder of its time in the line. The "D's" 30-year reign was the longest of any model John Deere tractor.

The 11 tractors photographed in front of the John Deere Tractor Company in Waterloo, Iowa, shown on the following spread, were all equipped with dual rear wheels so they had plenty of flotation for working in the Dust Bowl areas of Kansas in the 1930s.

MODEL GP

The Model "GP" Tractor was the second generation to bear the John Deere name. The "GP" model designation stood for "general purpose." Actually, the "GP" was preceded by the Model "C," but after 110 were built, most were recalled, modified and reissued as "GP" Tractors.

The "GP" did not replace the Model "D"; instead, it provided farmers—particularly in the Corn Belt—with a tractor with increased versatility. While the "D" was limited to drawbar and belt work, the "GP" was designed to accommodate integrally mounted equipment. The "GP" had an exclusive feature that enabled the operator to lift integral equipment mechanically with a pedal. This mechanical power lift was a John Deere "first" and was quickly copied by competitive tractor manufacturers.

The "GP" was introduced in 1928 and stayed in the line until 1935. It was smaller, lighter weight and less powerful than the Model "D." It had 10 horsepower at the drawbar and 20 horsepower at the belt at 950 revolutions per minute. It also had a 520-rpm PTO.

The "GP" had a standard wheel tread and was considered a 2-plow tractor. It also was called a 3-row tractor, because it had an arched, high-clearance, front axle that enabled it to straddle one row while cultivating the rows on either side.

John Deere introduced a 3-row integral planter and a 3-row integral cultivator for the "GP" Tractor. With this equipment, one man in one day could plant 30 to 40 acres or cultivate 24 to 40 acres. In comparison, it would take four men with single-row cultivators and eight horses to work the same acreage.

Also introduced for use with the "GP" was an integral sweep rake for picking up and stacking loose hay or straw, and an integral sicklebar mower with a 7-foot cutterbar. The mower was driven by the PTO and raised or lowered by the foot-operated mechanical lift. At a travel speed of 3 to 4 miles per hour, one man could mow 20 to 30 acres in a day.

Individual rear-wheel brakes enabled the operator to turn a "GP" quickly at row end. The turning radius without brakes was 8 feet. The "GP" had three forward speeds: 2⅓, 3⅛ and 4⅓ miles per hour. Reverse speed was 2 miles per hour.

For its size and weight (3,600 lb.), the "GP" had excellent lugging ability. This was due, of course, to the horizontal, heavy-duty, 2-cylinder engine and low engine speed (950 rpm). The "GP" was an economical tractor to operate because the engine was designed to burn efficiently kerosene and other low-grade, low-cost fuels.

With all its mechanical advantages, the "GP" was not as popular in the South as it was in the Midwest. The 3-row concept was the drawback. Cotton farmers wanted 2- or 4-row equipment. In response to this demand, John Deere introduced the "GP" Wide-Tread Tractor. It stayed in the line from 1929 to 1933.

The Wide-Tread had a longer rear axle than the "GP," giving it a 76-inch rear wheel tread and enabling the drive wheels to straddle two 36- to 42-inch rows. It also had a tricycle front end with two large-diameter, self-cleaning wheels that fit neatly between two rows. When operating on beds or ridges, the front wheels could be reversed to put the concave surfaces on the inside. Then John Deere introduced 2- and 4-row integral corn and

As the letter designation suggests, the "GP" was designed to be a general purpose tractor. It was smaller, lighter in weight and less powerful than the Model "D." It also cost $200 less, which doesn't seem like much today; but in 1929, $200 was 20 percent of the total price. At right is a "GP" with a 1-row corn picker.

cotton planters and 2- and 4-row integral cultivators for use with the Wide-Tread.

In 1932, the Wide-Tread hood was tapered to give the operator a better view forward for cultivating. Advertising literature that year noted that the improved visibility was "fully equal to that of any horse-drawn cultivator." The steering was repositioned so it passed over the hood and down the front of the radiator.

This later model Wide-Tread had a seat mounted on an adjustable cushion spring as a means of improving operator comfort. It also had controls positioned where the operator could reach them conveniently to change travel speed without taking his eyes off his work.

There were different versions of the "GP" and "GP" Wide-Tread. A "GPO" Tractor was built for handling both orchard and field work. It had modified fenders, extra shielding and a "laid down" air intake and exhaust. The seat support was repositioned on some "GPOs" so the operator sat lower to the ground and was shielded by the fenders from low-hanging branches.

Some "GP" Wide-Tread Tractors were built in 1930 with a slightly narrower rear axle so they could be used in potato fields in the Northeast. These were called "Series P" Tractors. Later an inset rear wheel was designed so the "GP" Wide-Tread had a wheel tread of 68 inches without narrowing the axle. This rear-wheel option eliminated the need for the "Series P" version.

The versatility, successful performance, and wide farmer acceptance of the "GPs" set the stage for John Deere's next big step in the farm tractor market: the introduction of the Model "A" and "B" Tractors.

There were many versions of the "GP" Tractor. The two above are "Series P" Wide-Treads with a 68-inch rear-wheel tread designed for working in potato fields. These two tractors have consecutive serial numbers. The one with cultivator has the original steel wheels. The other tractor was farmer-converted for rubber tires.

The original "GP" was not popular with southern cotton farmers, so John Deere introduced the Wide-Tread version, shown at right. Note the large-diameter double front wheels. When working on beds or ridges, these front wheels could be reversed to put the concave surfaces on the inside.

On the opposite page is a "GP" pulling a 2-bottom moldboard plow; this was about all the plow it could handle in normal Midwestern soil conditions.

JOHN DEERE
GENERAL PURPOSE
FARM TRACTOR

The GENERAL PURPOSE TRACTOR OF STANDARD DESIGN THAT DOES ALL FARM WORK WITHIN ITS POWER RANGE INCLUDING PLANTING AND CULTIVATING

Reproduced at left is a 2-page illustration from a 1929 "GP" Tractor sales folder. Actually, the tractor shown was a Model "C." However, shortly after its introduction, the "C" model designation was changed to "GP," because "C" and "D" sounded too much alike on the early telephones, resulting in confusion with dealer tractor orders. This illustration shows the wide variety of jobs this versatile power unit was designed to handle; it also points out the reason why this model was called a General Purpose Tractor.

Shown below is a 1931 Model "GP" Tractor. Note how the exhaust and air-intake extend well above the tractor hood, as compared to the tractor shown at left. The air-intake was raised to assure that clean air was pulled into the engine in dusty field conditions, thus extending the life of the engine. The exhaust was raised for the comfort of the operator: less noise and fumes. Also, the engine sparks were discharged upward instead of downward into flammable stubble. This tractor also is equipped with a belt pulley dust guard for added operator comfort.

The close-up photograph below is of the "GP" front axle. The high-arch design distinguished the "GP" from the "D" and provided crop clearance when the tractor was equipped with a 3-row cultivator.

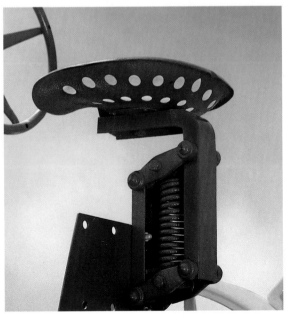

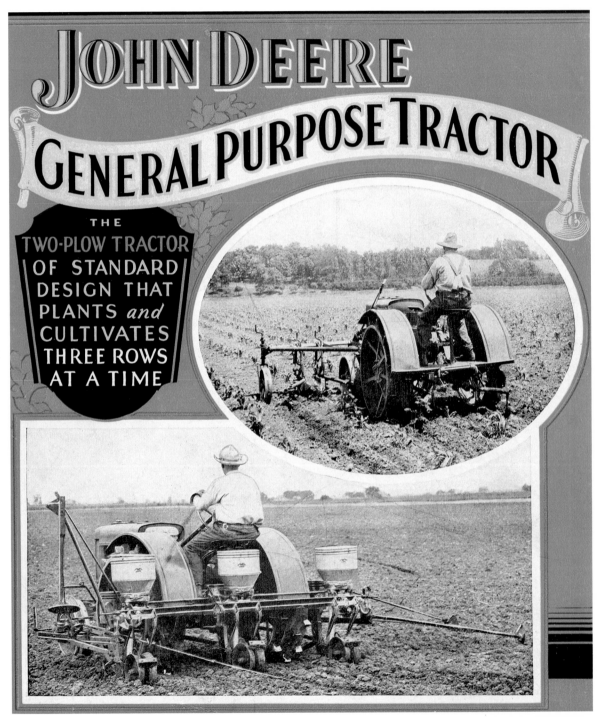

JOHN DEERE
GENERAL PURPOSE TRACTOR

THE
TWO-PLOW TRACTOR
OF STANDARD
DESIGN THAT
PLANTS *and*
CULTIVATES
THREE ROWS
AT A TIME

mproving operator comfort was an early concern of John Deere tractor engineers. Shown on the opposite page, lower left, is a seat suspension system used on the 1932 and 1933 "GP" Wide-Treads. This parallel linkage system under spring tension helped to smooth the rough ride of steel wheels on hard-packed gravel roads. The multiple leaf-spring suspension shown on the "GP" Wide-Tread below was a more common arrangement, but it was somewhat like sitting on the end of a springboard.

The seat suspension system shown on the opposite page, upper left, was used on the Model "C" Tractor. This must be the reason why many farmers preferred to operate their tractors while standing.

Note the reference to 3-row planting and cultivating on the cover of the early "GP" sales folder at left. This 3-row approach proved to be less popular with farmers than the 2-row system that preceded it and the 4-row approach that eventually replaced it.

Commercial orchard growers liked the size and power of the "GP" Tractor, but they needed a tractor that could be operated more conveniently under low-hanging branches. John Deere's response was the "GPO." It had a lower operator station. Then the Lindeman Company of Yakima, Washington, decided that the apple growers in the hilly Yakima Valley really needed a "GPO" on crawler treads. That's how the 1935 "GPO-Lindeman," shown at right, came into existence. Later crawler conversions used the "BO" chassis.

In the close-up photograph below is the flat head of the horizontal, 2-cylinder engine in a "GP" Tractor. Also shown below are two of the front-wheel options on a "GP" Wide-Tread Tractor. The concave wheels in the center were popular with southern farmers who planted cotton and corn on beds or ridges. The wheels on the right were popular with corn and soybean farmers in the Midwest.

The "GP" Wide-Tread shown on the opposite page was one of the last ones built. Note how the steering mechanism runs over the hood and in front of the radiator, as it does on the Model "A" that replaced the Wide-Tread. Two large mounting "holes" in the frame and the drop rear axles are characteristic of the Wide-Tread.

MODEL A

ate in 1933, advertising literature proclaimed: "John Deere's latest contribution to the great farming industry—the new John Deere Model 'A' General Purpose Two-Plow Tractor. This Model 'A' is a brand new tractor—new in its greater adaptability—new in its wider range of utility—new in the array of outstanding features it contains—new in greater economy of operation." That was a very, very promising forecast for a tractor that wouldn't be built for several months yet. But also prophetic.

This revolutionary tractor more than lived up to its advance billing, with more than 292,000 built! They came in a wide variety of configurations from a single front wheel row-crop version to a streamlined orchard style.

This versatility and adaptability, more than the 20-year span during which the "A" came off the factory assembly line, spelled this model's tremendous success. Earlier tractors had been designed to work in rows 40 to 42 inches apart, that being the amount of space needed for a horse.

Since tractors began pulling the equipment built for horses, they were designed with fixed tread that limited farmers to certain row spacings. This also limited the attaching points available to equipment designers. Plows, which worked to the right of the tractors, developed considerable side draft.

The "A" overcame these limitations, by offering adjustable rear-wheel tread, a one-piece transmission case that provided high under-axle clearance,

Under shiny styling, this 1950s "A," pulling an automatic-tie baler, closely resembled the "A" introduced more than 15 years earlier. Above, the hitch as well as the PTO shaft were located on the tractor centerline. This overcame side draft and considerably eased operator steering effort while plowing.

and by aligning the hitch and powershaft on the centerline of the tractor.

Rear wheels could be slid in or out on splines in the axles. This permitted wheel spacings from 56 to 84 inches (center to center).

For plowing, wheels could be set at 56 inches. This centered the plow behind the tractor and eliminated side draft problems. They could be set at 68 inches for working in potatoes, 76 inches for cotton, 80 inches for corn, or any setting in between for other specialized situations. Variable wheel spacings also permitted offset configurations for special applications, such as irregular row spacings and for the operator who preferred to sit more directly over one of the rows being cultivated.

On the early "A's," four forward speeds permitted the operator to select the best travel rate for the conditions. Speeds of 2⅓ and 3⅓ miles per hour were suited for heavier drawbar jobs, such as plowing, disking, bedding, planting, harvesting and corn picking. The higher 4¾ mile per hour speed was handy for seedbed finishing. (In 1940, the "A" was equipped with a 6-speed transmission.)

The newly available "low-pressure pneumatic tires" (called "balloon tires" in the 1934 price list) allowed use of the 6¾ mile per hour top speed for road transport.

While the "A" General Purpose version proved popular in areas where farmers raised crops in rows, grain farmers asked for a tractor that would provide them with the same economy, productivity and versatility. Thus came the standard tread "AR," with widespread front wheels and fixed rear tread, for general field work on the plains. Narrow and wide front tread, orchard, high-clearance, and industrial styles followed.

The "A" also inspired a little brother, the "B," which you can read about in the next chapter.

Preceding spread: During its two-decade lifetime in the John Deere line, many different configurations of the "A" were produced (in fact, too many to show in one photo.) In addition, the "A" received modern styling to enhance its reputation for engineering excellence. The "A's" built between 1934 and 1938 are considered unstyled. Generally, those produced from 1939 through 1946 are styled and those from then until 1953 were late styled. Clockwise from top left: Styled "AW"; late styled "AN" and "A"; "AI"; unstyled "AWH," 1934 "A's" on rubber and steel wheels (with road bands for transport), "AN" and "AW"; "AO" Streamlined. The "W" and "N" stood for wide and narrow tread, "I" for industrial, "H" for high clearance, and "O" for orchard.

This spread: When they first became available, many farmers were skeptical about rubber tires. Early "A's," such as the "AN" and "AW" at the far right, helped prove the worth of smooth-riding, traction-increasing rubber tires. Even then, steel wheels didn't disappear totally until the 1950s.

Right: All of the tractors in this book shared a common characteristic . . . a 2-cylinder engine. The pages reproduced here from a 1936 brochure clearly explain why.

Below: The distinctive lettering cast into the rear-axle housing dressed up production models and gives restorers great satisfaction of accomplishment when completed perfectly. Oftentimes, restorations are more precise than when the tractors were brand new.

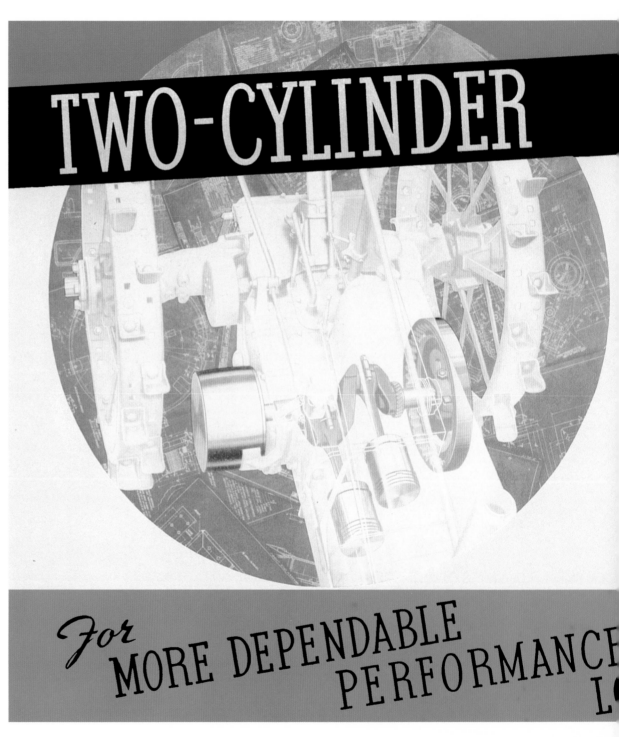

TWO-CYLINDER

For MORE DEPENDABLE PERFORMANCE

ENGINE DESIGN

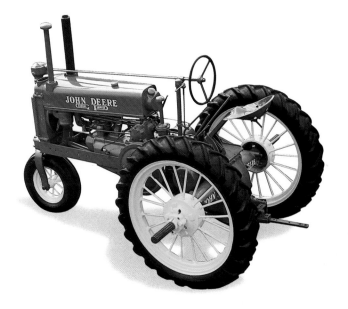

JOHN DEERE tractors stand alone in farm tractor engine design: they have only two cylinders. The ever-increasing swing to John Deere tractors is ample proof of the soundness, the practicability of this design.

You know that the simpler a tractor can be made the less chance there will be for trouble and field delays. The John Deere is by far the simplest tractor on the market. totally free from hundreds of parts that are necessary in other tractors. And, in addition, the same simplicity that has made it possible to reduce the total number of parts also permits making the remaining parts larger, heavier, stronger—better able to stand up under the grueling strains of farm work.

The John Deere two-cylinder tractor not only gives you as much and in many cases more power than other tractors of similar size and weight, but, in addition, two-cylinder engine design gives you more dependable performance and longer life.

Along with dependability and long life, you want economy in the tractor you buy. John Deere tractors save you money on the biggest single expense item in the operation of a tractor—fuel. Two-cylinder engine design is especially adapted to the successful burning of the low-cost fuels.

You want a tractor that's easy to understand, to operate, to care for. The cylinders in a John Deere are *horizontal*, with the crankshaft *crosswise* to the main frame. Because of this design, all working parts are accessible and all adjustments can be made from a standing position.

The exclusive John Deere two-cylinder engine is specially built for heavy-duty farm work . . . it gives you the things you want most in your tractor.

NGER LIFE *and* GREATER ECONOMY

Far page: Top right; although crude by current standards, the early "A" offered a more comfortable spring-loaded seat. It also introduced hydraulic power for lifting heavier implements with considerably less effort.

Top center; magneto ignition and hand starting was the norm before electric starting became available in 1940. Top left; the all-fuel "A" carried two fuel tanks, a small one for gasoline and a larger one for less refined, cheaper fuel. The rounded 1-gallon tank in the upper right of this photo provided gasoline for starting the engine. After the engine warmed up, distillate or other low grade fuel was burned from a 14-gallon tank under the hood. Bottom; this beautifully restored pair, a 1936 "AN" and "AW," boast consecutive serial numbers.

Near right: This cover of the first Model "A" brochure reveals that adjustable wheel tread (along with other features such as hydraulic lift and more attaching points) permitted implement engineers to design equipment for specific agricultural needs. The tractor illustrated here was a pre-production model and was not exactly the same as those that came off the assembly line when production began in the spring of 1934.

The New
JOHN DEERE Model "A"
GENERAL PURPOSE
TRACTOR
with ADJUSTABLE TREAD

JOHN DEERE
GENERAL PURPOSE

-and One-Man Working Equipment Built for Use on Southern Farms.

COMFORTABLE. Large, bucket-type seat rides on a spring-mounted, channel-steel, support. Roomy platform enables operator to sit or stand at will.

EASY TO OPERATE. All controls—clutch, throttle, gear shift, etc.—are within easy reach of the operator from the tractor seat.

VENTILATED CRANKCASE. Breather and ventilator maintain forced circulation of **clean** air through crankcase—remove gases and vapors.

PROPER LINE OF DRAFT. Swinging drawbar is permanently located. Has a wide range of adjustment vertically and horizontally.

EFFICIENT POWER TAKE-OFF. Furnished as standard equipment on John Deere general purpose tractors. Runs in a bath of oil.

AUTOMATIC LUBRICATION OF TRANSMISSION AND DIFFERENTIAL. Gears are fully enclosed and run in a bath of **clean** oil.

The callouts captioning this cutaway view capsulize the advanced thinking that went into the early "A." Each of these features offered important practical benefits to farmers who were switching from horses to mechanical power, as well as to those who were already using less-refined tractors.

Far right, top: "Narrow" tractors with a single front wheel, were perfect for work in closely spaced rows. Far right, bottom: Introduction of adjustable rear wheel spacing catapulted the "A" into prominence among row-crop farmers. This John Deere innovation made possible infinite tread settings as close as 56 inches and as wide as 84 inches. The widest spacings were accomplished by reversing the wheels or moving them from one side of the tractor to the other, so that the hubs faced inward.

VISIBLE GAUGES. Oil gauge registers oil pressure; water temperature gauge tells operator when to adjust radiator shutter.

CLEAN AIR TO ENGINE. Oil wash-down air cleaner is efficient in its operation and easy to service.

SHOCK-PROOF, AUTOMOTIVE-TYPE STEERING. Irreversible worm and gear sector with adjustable eccentric provides quick, easy control.

PROPER ENGINE TEMPERATURE. Radiator shutter, controlled from tractor seat, regulates temperature for most economical operation.

Model "A"

POSITIVE AIR FLOW THROUGH RADIATOR. Fan is gear-driven—no belt to slip, cause trouble, and require replacement.

POSITIVE ENGINE LUBRICATION. Pump forces oil **under pressure** through filter to main and connecting rod bearings, piston pins. Other parts automatically lubricated.

LONGER LIFE. Crankshaft, connecting rods, pistons, axles, gears, and other parts are built larger, heavier, stronger, for more years of service.

AUTOMATIC TEMPERATURE CONTROL. John Deere thermo-siphon system is fully effective under all loads and temperatures. Simple—no water pump or thermostat.

Because relatively few were built each year, two-cylinder tractor enthusiasts are particularly fond of specialty tractors. Orchard models are a prime example. These tractors were lowered and shrouded for work between closely spaced fruit and nut trees, and underneath their branches.

The late-unstyled "AO" pictured on these pages was built in 1946. Notice how the entire tractor hugs the ground, how the muffler lays horizontally alongside the engine, how the water and fuel caps as well as the air intakes are all carefully shielded, and how the operator controls are shortened and protected. Even the seat is mounted at a different angle, to position the driver lower than he would be on an ordinary standard-tread tractor.

The late styled "AR," right, produced from 1949 into 1953, previewed the look of John Deere tractors to follow in the 1950s. The even more eye-catching "AO" below and on the next page was a squatty "AR" with extensive branch-protecting shielding. These two versions were the last Model "A's" produced. They came off the line until May of 1953, within a few months of completing two full decades of "A" production. As futuristic as the 1949 Model "AO" was, the "AO" Streamlined (below right) had established futuristic styling 12 years earlier. It was slightly smaller in physical size and about 20 percent smaller in horsepower than the late-styled "AO."

A Real Orchard Tractor . . .
in both appearance and performance

Above: Here's the Model "AO" Streamlined Orchard Tractor equipped with low-pressure, rubber tires which are special equipment. Notice the heavy, cast rear wheels. This wheel construction eliminates spokes and provides proper traction in most conditions without the use of wheel weights. This tractor is regularly furnished with steel wheels as shown on the tractor at the right.

Left: Notice the smooth, rounded, full skirted fenders, big comfortable seat, foot brakes, handy position of all controls, shielded power take-off, and easily adjusted drawbar. Everything is low-down—only the operator's head projects above the cowl.

[4]

Above: Here is the Model "AO" Streamlined Tractor equipped with regular steel wheels. Notice the radiator guard, the absence of all projections and sharp angles, the smooth, rounded corners.

At its highest point, the top of the cowl, this tractor stands only 53 inches high.

Right: This photograph will give you some idea of the narrow, compact design of the Model "AO" Streamlined Tractor. With steel drive wheels it is only 55¾ inches wide—ideal for vineyards with 10-foot row centers, for hopyards with only 7-foot row centers. Notice that the belt pulley is right on the end of the crankshaft for maximum power.

[5]

During its lifetime in the line, the venerable "A" had grown in power from 16 to 26½ horsepower at the drawbar. This significantly increased work capacity, of course, as illustrated by this 1950 picture of an "A" with 4-row planter in a large field.

Early tractor-design objectives emphasized versatility, dependability, and economy. But late in the 1930s, styling also became a major objective...because well-engineered products should also look good. Appearance became a yardstick of quality. So John Deere retained noted industrial designer Henry Dreyfuss to ensure the desired marriage of esthetics and performance. The impressive grille styling, above left, represents the results of his first efforts and began appearing late in 1938.

But esthetics certainly wasn't the only concern of John Deere engineers. Mechanical modernization was also ongoing. A good example is exclusive "knee action" Roll-O-Matic front wheels (left). This welcome option became available in 1947 and automatically transferred up-and-down movement equally through both front wheels. Thus, the effect of one wheel going over a 4-inch bump or rock, or through a 4-inch depression, was the same as if both wheels rode over a 2-inch obstruction.

V for "Victory" became a popular gesture during World War II. As men left for military service, many women ran the farms at home with easy-to-operate tractors like this Model "A." This painting, one of a series done by Walter Haskell Hinton, first showed up on the 1945 John Deere calendar. While a hand-operated clutch was standard equipment on every "A," hydraulic power was introduced as an option in 1934 and improved considerably during the "A" period (bottom). Below, this attractive emblem distinguished the late-styled "AR" and "AO."

HAND CLUTCH

The John Deere hand clutch is a mighty important convenience feature. It eliminates the inconvenience of mounting the tractor to engage or disengage the clutch when working on belt jobs. It gives you complete control of the tractor while standing on the platform—there's no need to sit down to operate the clutch. It makes hitching to implements a one-man job. You'll want this feature in your next tractor.

Engaging the clutch of a Model "A" from the ground to operate a belt-driven machine.

MODEL B

Certainly, the "A" was a leader in tractor popularity. But not the only leader. Its "smaller brother," the "B," was even more popular. More than 306,000 of this model were built from 1935 through 1952. Such enthusiastic acceptance made the "B" the most popular John Deere tractor ever. Its success wasn't because of advancements over the "A." Instead, it was the perfect size for greater numbers of farmers. Advertising materials announcing the new "B" quoted the appeals of small farm owners: "Give me a tractor built along the same lines, that will fit my small farm so that I can do away with horses." Larger farmers added, "Give me a small John Deere tractor so I can add it to my tractor equipment and thereby do my lighter work at lower cost." The text went on to describe the "B" as "about two-thirds the size of the Model 'A' in power, weight and dimensions, but with all of the advanced features of the Model 'A.' It pulls a 16-inch plow, a 1-bottom middlebreaker, a 2-row planter, 2-row cultivator, or similar loads."

Those advanced features included "the ability to operate on low-grade fuels—effortless vision—easy steering—and adjustable rear wheel tread." Another advancement carried along to the "B" was using hydraulic power to lift implements. Hydraulic lift, which replaced the mechanical lift system on the "GP," permitted raising bigger loads with considerably less effort. Using a simple foot lever, the operator raised and lowered implements effortlessly, whether the tractor was moving or standing still. Hydraulics also provided a cushioned drop of the implement.

This large photograph, taken in 1935, shows considerable advancement in picking corn as compared with 20 years earlier. Clearly, horses were being relegated to a secondary role in farming. Above: By the time the late-styled "B" (and "A") were introduced in 1947, 2-row mounted corn pickers were commonplace . . . soon to be followed by even more-advanced self-propelled corn combines.

One of the main reasons farmers chose John Deere tractors when they switched from horses was operating economy. The "B" shined here, too. First, its small size made it low in initial cost.

Next, like its bigger brother, the "B" could burn inexpensive fuels such as distillate, fuel oil, and furnace oil. According to the early advertising literature: "Saving $1 to $2 a day in fuel costs is the rule rather than the exception." Besides the efficiencies from burning cheaper fuel, farmers realized additional fuel savings because the "B" weighed considerably less than other tractors of the day. When introduced, the nimble "B" weighed only 2,455 pounds, a clear indication of its refined design.

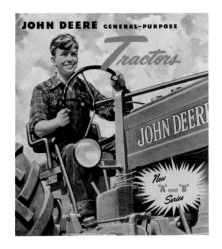

Also, "B" owners realized operating economies from the durable, valve-in-head 2-cylinder engine. Sales folders touted the need for only two pistons instead of four or six, four pairs of valves and valve springs instead of eight or 12. "Upkeep costs are extremely low. You can make the ordinary adjustments yourself at a great saving in time and expense."

The advertising went on to point out that this "unequalled simplicity is carried through the entire tractor . . . placing the belt pulley on the crankshaft, the straight-line transmission, the flywheel starting, the thermosiphon cooling, in practically every moving part. This simplicity, which makes hundreds of parts unnecessary, results in heavier, more rugged parts which last longer."

Several other design advancements set the early "B," and the "A," apart from ordinary tractors. For example, a force-feed oiling system thoroughly lubricated all parts of the engine . . . a unique oil filter used a metal filtering element to remove foreign particles from the oil . . . a one-piece, oil-tight and dust-proof case kept gears and shafts in perfect alignment and automatically oiled.

The simple, practical design of these two tractors proved so popular that John Deere made it available in a larger version, and also in a smaller version, which you can read about in upcoming chapters.

Depending on the acreage, some farmers used the "B" as a secondary tractor while others used it as their primary tractor. But large and small farmers alike appreciated the almost 7-mph transport speed that the "B" and a roller-bearing equipped, pneumatic-tired wagon brought to them.

The bird's-eye view below is of a 1935 Model "B" Garden Tractor, one of the first "BNs" built. Because many "market gardeners, truck farmers, or market growers" worked expensive land, they raised little or no feed and didn't have cheap pasture land. So horses were especially inconvenient and expensive for them. However, they still wanted to plow deep and prepare their land even better than the general farmer. Thus, John Deere designed for them this narrow-tired, single front-wheel "B" Garden Tractor and a complete line of matching tillage, planting and cultivating equipment.

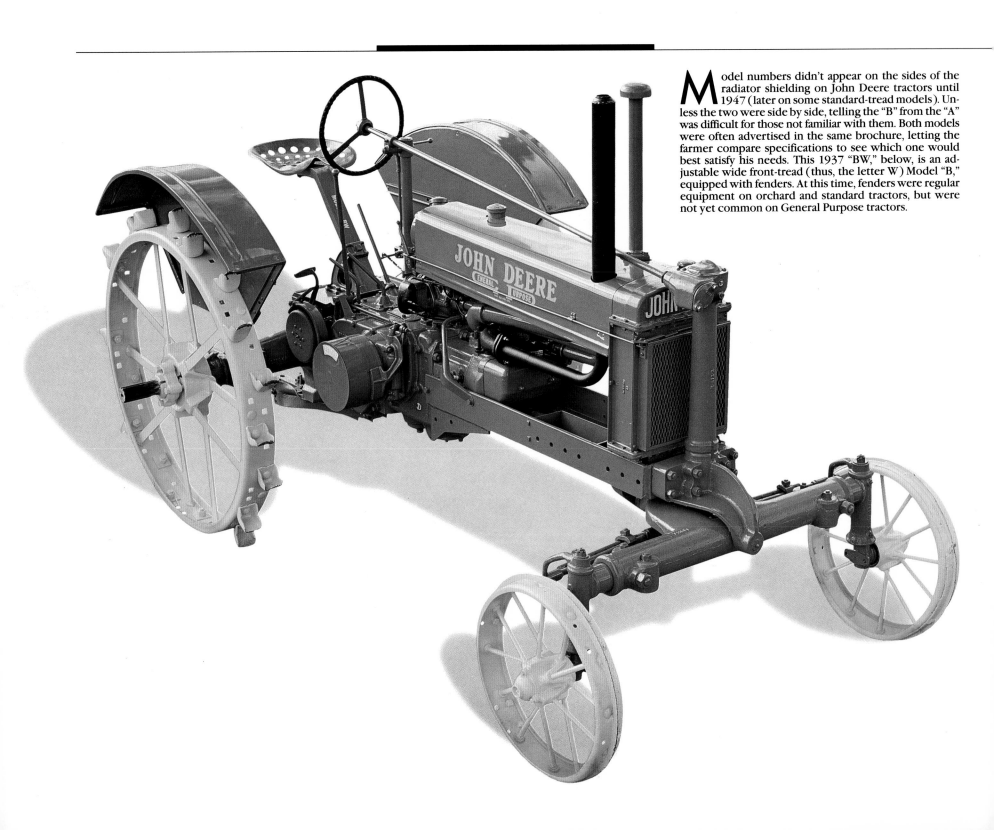

M odel numbers didn't appear on the sides of the radiator shielding on John Deere tractors until 1947 (later on some standard-tread models). Unless the two were side by side, telling the "B" from the "A" was difficult for those not familiar with them. Both models were often advertised in the same brochure, letting the farmer compare specifications to see which one would best satisfy his needs. This 1937 "BW," below, is an adjustable wide front-tread (thus, the letter W) Model "B," equipped with fenders. At this time, fenders were regular equipment on orchard and standard tractors, but were not yet common on General Purpose tractors.

JOHN DEERE Models A and B

GENERAL PURPOSE GP TRACTORS

THE MODEL "A" TRACTOR FOR AVERAGE FARM WORK
THE MODEL "B" TRACTOR FOR THE LIGHTER FARM JOBS

• SPECIFICATIONS •
MODEL B

Power Capacity—Handles the load ordinarily pulled by 4 horses.

Engine—2-cylinder cast en bloc, valve-in-head. Bore 4-1/4 inches. Stroke 5-1/4 inches. Rated speed loaded—1150 R.P.M.

Crankshaft—2-1/4-inch drop-forged stock, special quality steel.

Connecting Rods—Special quality steel, drop-forged, floating on piston pin.

Lubrication—Pressure system, with oil filter.

Cooling—Thermo-siphon with air fan, gear- and shaft-driven (no water pump nor belts).

Air-Cleaner—Oil wash-down type with vertical stack.

Carburetor—John Deere natural-draft system with 1-1/2-inch carburetor of dual adjustment.

Ignition—High-tension magneto with enclosed automatic impulse coupling.

Governor—Enclosed John Deere fly-ball type.

Clutch—Two 8-inch dry disks, locking in and out.

Belt Pulley—10-5/8-inch diameter x 6-inch face, mounted on crankshaft. 1150 R.P.M. Belt speed—3200 F.P.M.

Transmission—Selective type, spur gear. Gears forged steel, cut and heat-treated. Four speeds forward: First—2-1/3; Second—3; Third—4-3/4; Fourth—6-1/4; Reverse—3-1/2 M.P.H.

Final Drive—Forged steel gears, cut and heat-treated.

Rear Axles—2-3/8-inch diameter, alloy steel, heat-treated.

Wheels:
Front—22-inch diameter x 3-1/4-inch face, steel tires, dust-proof bearings.
Drive—48-inch diameter x 5-1/4-inch face, steel tires.

Fuel Tank Capacity—Approximately 14 gallons distillate with 1-gallon gasoline tank.

Water Capacity—5-1/2 gallons.

Crank Case Capacity—6 quarts, with 1 additional when oil filter has been drained, recommended.

Transmission Case Capacity—5 gallons, or to level of filler plug.

Power Take-Off—1-1/8-inch spline—553 R.P.M.

Bearings:
Crankshaft—2 main, removable bronze-backed, babbitt-lined, 2-1/4-inch diameter x 2-1/2 inches long. 2 connecting rods, centrifugally spun in rod, 2-1/4-inch diameter x 2 inches long, bronze-bushed for piston pin.
Cam Shaft—2 plain.
Transmission—5 ball, 3 roller, 4 taper roller, 2 bronze.
Belt Pulley—1 roller, 1 bronze.
Governor—2 self-adjusting ball, 1 thrust ball.
Fan—2 self-adjusting ball.
Rear Axle—4 taper roller.
Front Wheels—4 taper roller.
Steering—2 taper and 2 plain.

Dimensions:
Over-All Length—122 inches.
Width—85 inches.
Height—Top of radiator—56 inches.
Wheel Base—80 inches.
Turning Radius—8 feet.
Tread—Adjustable 56 inches to 80 inches.
Drawbar—Vertical range, 9 inches to 13 inches.
Fore and aft, 8-1/2 inches.
Horizontal range, 24 inches.

Shipping Weight—Approximately 2765 pounds.

The farmyard portrait at the left shows the "BR," a standard-tread version of the "B." It was designed for use in wheat country and other applications not requiring adjustable wheel tread. Introduced along with the General Purpose "B" in 1935, the "BR" changed little until discontinued in 1947. Equipped with a single front wheel, the General Purpose "B" became the "BN" (below). This statement from the 1935 sales brochure places this tractor into perspective size-wise: "While the Model 'B' Tractor weighs less than two good horses, it will do the work of four."

F ar left: The "BO" Lindeman is an orchard wheel tractor chassis mounted on a tracked undercarriage, for use in hillside orchards and woodlots. Upper left: This rare (apparently only six were built) BW-40 could work in row spacings as narrow as 20 inches, and in crops such as beets on beds 40 inches apart. The bug-eyed tractor below was one of the last "BRs" built, in 1947. Its high-mounted headlights and rear "equipment" light (lower left) allowed farmers to put in extra hours in the field when conditions made it advisable. Bottom right: This close-up photo shows the front hitch and oscillating front axle on a "standard" tractor. Bottom center: Before electric starters, tractors had to be started by hand—by turning the flywheel. Opening the petcock next to the spark plug released cylinder compression for easier starting.

By the time the "B" retired from the John Deere tractor line in 1952, it was a considerably matured tractor from the version born in 1935. Attractive styling, comfortable seats, increased horsepower (from 9-hp when introduced, to 19-hp for the gasoline version when it left the line), rubber tires and numerous other improvements all occurred while the "B" was "growing up."

Below: Rubber tires were scarce during World War II. So even though most farmers wanted tractors on "rubber," they had to settle for steel because tires weren't available. This is a "wartime" Model "B," built in 1941.

Right: Wouldn't any farm youngster have loved to have had Santa bring this shiny new, 1952 beauty for Christmas? (Well, for Dad, anyway!)

Far right: The "new" models being announced in this advertising material were the styled "B" and "A" in 1938. They received further styling refinements and horsepower increases again in 1947.

GREATER VALUE than Ever Before in the new JOHN DEERE

MODELS "A" and "B" TRACTORS

HERE they are—two new John Deere general purpose tractors—a new Model "A" and a new, *more powerful* Model "B". These tractors, styled for tomorrow, offer even better vision . . . greater comfort . . . added convenience features . . . offer greater value than ever before.

Built with the Qualities You Want Most

You're looking for the tractor that will do the most work for the longest time and at the lowest possible cost. Such a tractor should offer the maximum in certain fundamental qualities—adaptability to your power jobs, dependability, long life, economy, ease of operation, and comfort.

John Deere general purpose tractors are outstanding in *all* of these qualities—the qualities you want most in a farm tractor.

From radiator to drawbar—down to the last bolt and nut—everything has been designed to serve a definite, practical purpose. The simple, two-cylinder engine . . . the straight-line transmission of power . . . the sensitive governor that controls the engine at *all* speeds . . . the positive, force-feed pressure lubrication system . . . the position and design of seat, platform, fuel tank, brakes, steering gear, controls, clutch . . . the hydraulic power lift . . . the full adjustability of the rear wheels for all row crops. . . the wide variety of integral working equipment, and a host of other features . . . all form an exclusive combination of advantages not found on other tractors.

The new Models "A" and "B" give you all of the time-tried and field-proved features which farmers have enjoyed in previous John Deere general purpose tractors plus other features which mean even greater value.

After you have read this booklet, drop in at your John Deere dealer's and ask for a demonstration. Drive one of these new tractors. Then make any comparisons you would like to make. We feel certain you'll agree that a John Deere general purpose is the greatest tractor value on the market today.

they're TOMORROW'S TRACTORS Today

MODEL G

Utilizing mechanical horsepower instead of "horses" power greatly increased the amount of work a farm family could handle. Naturally, this greater work capacity led to increasingly larger farms. In turn, those bigger spreads required larger tractors. John Deere watched and reacted to this trend by introducing the Model "G" in 1938. The "G" brought full 3-plow power for all field and row-crop work to large cotton and corn growers, and to grain farmers who also raised some cotton or corn.

Promotional materials of the day stated what a farmer could do with this powerful general purpose tractor. In 10 hours, for example, he could plow up to 12 acres ... cover 25 to 35 acres with a 10-foot double disk or 75 to 100 acres with a 21-foot single disk ... list or bed 35 to 50 acres ... plant as high as 60 acres with an integral 4-row cotton planter or drawn corn planter ... cultivate from 40 to 60 acres with a 4-row cultivator ... cut 25 to 35 acres with a power mower ... harvest 40 to 50 or more acres with a 10-foot grain binder ... pick from 10 to 18 acres with a 2-row corn picker ... pull a 2-row potato digger ... or operate a threshing machine with 28-inch threshing cylinder. Having just moved out of the horse era, only the most forward-thinking row-crop farmers could comprehend such "Clydesdale" and "Belgian" accomplishments. This kind of ability made ordinary tractors appear like "Shetland Ponies."

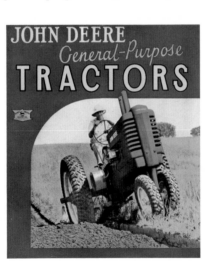

Except for physical size, the "G" looked just like the "A" and "B." But that was only during its year of introduction, because in 1939 the "A" and "B" became styled while the "G" remained unstyled. It was 1942 before the "G" sported Henry Dreyfuss styling. In fact, it wasn't even the "G" that was styled, because along with the fresh new look came mechanical modernization, including a 6-speeds-forward transmission, and renaming to "GM."

With additional redesign after World War II, the "GM" again became the "G." This happened in 1947, the same year that John Deere offered the company's first super-high-clearance tractor, called the "G" Hi-Crop. Prior to that, the "G" and "GM" had been available only in three versions; narrow (single front wheel), wide (widespread front wheels), and tricycle (front wheels close together).

Throughout its stay in the line the "G" was manufactured with an all-fuel engine. Referring to the 1939 sales materials offers the reason. "It is an indisputable fact that your fuel dollar buys more gallons of distillate than of regular or low-grade gasoline. While prices vary in different communities, at an average figure of eight cents for distillate, your fuel dollar buys twelve and one-half gallons of high grade distillate." This compared with getting only 8 gallons of regular gasoline for the dollar. That comparison used net prices, with tax deducted, but explained that since many states did not rebate gasoline tax the actual spread in cost could be materially more.

This comparison went on to point out that with regular gasoline, "... your dollar's worth of fuel does only 66.6 percent as much work as it does in a John Deere. In short, it's work per dollar, not work per gallon that counts."

Of course, the bigger the tractor the more fuel that tractor consumed ... so the greater the savings from burning lower-grade fuels in a big tractor such as the "G."

Prior to herbicides, weed-free corn was achieved by hoeing, pulling the weeds by hand, or by planting in check rows so the field could be cultivated both lengthways and crossways. Naturally, as farms grew bigger the only way to clean the larger fields was with bigger equipment. The "G" with a 4-row cultivator was ideal for such increased acreages. Even when viewed on the diagonal, isn't "checked" corn a beautiful sight? As discussed inside the brochure shown above, the "G" was available only as a General Purpose model, never as a standard tractor.

The last "G" built, serial number 64530, is pictured in restored splendor at the far left. Unlike the "A" and "B," the "G" continued to be built with a channel-type frame throughout its life. Compare the side frame, beneath the engine, in this picture with the new-style frame of the tractor on which Santa Claus is riding on page 68.

At the immediate left, this display room poster from 1938 invites prospects to experience firsthand what the "G" could do for them. By itself, a tractor of any size accomplishes little. Thus the need for a broad selection of implements sized to the power of that tractor.

The tractors pictured below span the 16-year lifetime of the "G" General Purpose Tractor. The skeleton steel-wheeled tractor is a 1938 "low-radiator" model, a description that signifies this was one of the earliest "Gs" produced. Continuing counterclockwise; an unstyled "G" with cast rear wheels, a "GM" built in 1945, a 1951 "G" Hi-Crop, and the end-of-production 1953 "G." To the right, a powerful "G" operating a forage harvester in heavy northwestern Illinois corn in 1951.

MODEL L

Having established a reputation for designing and building dependable "big" tractors, John Deere, in the mid-1930s, turned its attention to the power needs of the thousands of small-acreage farmers. These farmers were still relying on a team of horses or mules to supply their horsepower.

The Model "Y" was the first small-tractor prototype to be built in 1936 at the John Deere Wagon Works in Moline, Illinois. It was followed in early 1937 by the Model 62 of which there were fewer than 100 units produced. These 62 Tractors are easy to identify today because they have a large "JD" in the front casting under the radiator and in the rear-axle housing. Later in 1937, John Deere introduced the Model "L" to replace the 62. The "L" remained in the line until 1946.

The Model "L" was positioned in the marketplace and promoted as "the lightweight, economical tractor that handles all work ordinarily done with a team of horses." Although not known at the time, it also was John Deere's entry into the utility or "second-tractor" market.

The "L" continued the basic 2-cylinder engine design, but with a significant difference: The cylinders were vertical, instead of horizontal, as in all previous John Deere tractors. This simple, economical engine delivered 7 horsepower at the drawbar and 9 horsepower at the belt pulley at 1480 revolutions per minute. The "L" was designated a 1-plow tractor, because it pulled one 12-inch bottom, plowing 7 inches deep in second gear. Advertising at that time, however, made a special point about the work capacity of the "L," again comparing it to animal-produced horsepower: "IMPORTANT: It should be

remembered that while pulling loads ordinarily pulled with a team, the tractor turns out much more work in a day than a team of horses because of the faster speeds at which it works and the constant speed which it holds all day long."

The "L" had a standard automotive gearshift. The speed in first gear was 2½ miles per hour; in second, 3¾ miles per hour and in third, 6 miles per hour; the reverse speed was 3¾ miles per hour.

The "L" also had a foot-operated clutch, instead of a hand clutch as was standard on all other John Deere tractors. The engine, transmission and steering wheel were offset to the left of the tractor centerline. The operator's seat was positioned slightly to the right of center. This design, along with a tapered fuel tank and a "see through" twin-tubular skeleton frame, provided the operator with excellent visibility for cultivating. This feature was important to farmers who cultivated narrow-row vegetable crops.

The word "nimble" was frequently applied to the "L" Tractor because of its outstanding maneuverability. With the aid of individual rear-wheel brakes, it could turn in a tight 7-foot radius—a real time-saver when cultivating. An adjustable rear-wheel tread was another important feature. In the narrow 36-inch setting, the "L" could be used for cultivating crops planted in narrow rows. The normal 42-inch setting was used for plowing or cultivating corn. An extra-wide 54-inch tread was possible by reversing the offset or "dished" rear wheels. This setting was frequently used for check-planting corn or for extra stability when mowing on sidehills. Later model tractors also had an adjustable front-wheel tread.

A full line of implements and attachments gave the "L" considerable versatility. Integral equipment included a plow with one 12-inch bottom, 1-row cultivator that could be adapted for cultivating four 16-inch rows, spring-tooth harrow, and 3-, 4- or 5-narrow-row vegetable planters. Unfortunately, the

The unstyled 1938 Model "L" Tractor shown at left has the "dished" rear wheels set in the wide, 54-inch setting. This setting provided extra stability when mowing hilly golf courses; it also was used for planting corn in check rows. The "L" was light weight, economical and versatile.

"L" had no mechanical power or hydraulic lifting capability. All integral attachments had to be raised or lowered by hand; but then, so did all horse-drawn equipment. This was not considered a disadvantage at the time as it would be today.

Pull-type equipment included a 1-bottom plow, 5-foot disk harrow, 2-row corn planter, grain drill, hay mower, side-delivery rake and manure spreader.

The "L" had belt pulley power to operate a corn sheller, hammer mill, or portable grain elevator.

Along with several other John Deere tractors, the "L" received a face-lifting by the Dreyfuss industrial design group. In 1941, a second—slightly larger—small tractor was added to the John Deere line. It was the Model "LA."

The Model "LA" was positioned as a "second" or utility tractor. It had the added advantage of a 540 revolutions per minute PTO, more power, added weight and increased crop clearance. With 10 horsepower at the drawbar and nearly 13 horsepower at the belt pulley at 1850 revolutions per minute, the "LA" was frequently referred to as a "three-horse" tractor.

The "L" was the first John Deere tractor not to have a rubber tire option, as rubber tires were standard equipment. Optional equipment did include the belt pulley, fixed or swinging drawbar, electric starting and lights, rear-wheel weights, tire chains, mud lug wheels and PTO (on the "LA" only).

Farmers were encouraged by their John Deere dealers to consider the extra field working hours tractor power makes available: The time a horse farmer must spend each day caring for his horses both before and after work.

These small tractors were dropped from the line when production of the Model "M" began in 1946.

Clockwise, the tractors at right are a 1937 Model 62, an unstyled 1938 Model "L" with mud lug wheels attached to the rear wheels for added traction, a styled 1939 Model "L," a 1941 Model "LI" and a 1944 Model "LA." The Model 62 would be called a "pre-production" tractor; fewer than 100 were built as a prototype for the Model "L." Note the large yellow "JD" on the front casting under the radiator in the photograph at lower far right. A similar "JD" was cast into the rear axle housing. Both "JDs" were removed when the "L" replaced the 62. The Henry Dreyfuss styling that transformed the appearance of the Model "A," "B" and "D" Tractors also was applied to the Model "L." Late Model "L" and "LA" Tractors were equipped with the coil-spring seat suspension system (shown at upper far right) for added operator comfort.

Reproduced at right are two pages from a 1941 "L" and "LA" sales folder. Note how these two tractors are compared to a 2- and 3-horse team. Even after 25 years of tractor farming, many farmers prior to World War II still measured a tractor's power and performance to the more familiar capabilities of a team of horses. At upper far right is a 1937 Model "Y" Tractor, the predecessor of the Model 62. This tractor is a reproduction, built from an original set of plans. It is believed that all the original "Ys" were recalled by the Moline factory and destroyed. At lower far right is a close-up photograph of the front wheel used on the 62 and the unstyled Model "L." Note the "JD" on the wheelhub and simulated spoke wheel. Solid yellow wheels with large, plain green hubs were adapted for the styled models.

JOHN DEERE *Models*
COMPLETE POWER ON SMALL FARMS

"LA"

The Model "LA" . . . *Latest addition to the John Deere Line of 2-cylinder tractors . . . powered to pull all loads ordinarily handled with 3-horse team, such as one 16-inch plow or 5-foot double-action disk harrow . . . provides daily work capacity of 4 horses, because of its faster speeds and steadier work . . . available with electric starting and lights, belt pulley, and power take-off. Shown above with rear wheel weights.*

(4)

"L" and "LA" Tractors
..IDEAL HELPERS ON LARGE FARMS

"L"

The Model "L" ... *Similar in design and appearance to the Model "LA" but scaled down in weight, size, and power to pull all loads ordinarily handled with a 2-horse team, such as one 12-inch plow or 6-foot single-action disk harrow . . . daily work capacity of 3 horses . . . available with electric starting and lights and belt pulley. Between this tractor and the Model "LA", you can choose the power size that exactly fits your needs.*

(5)

This is the cover of a 1941 "L" and "LA" sales folder. Note the copy at the bottom. John Deere developed a wide variety of implements for these two small tractors: 1-bottom, 1- and 2-way plows; 1-row middle-breaker-bedder; 1- and 2-row planters with fertilizer attachments; 4-row vegetable planter; 1- and 2-row cultivators, sicklebar mower and side-delivery rake—all integrally mounted. Pull-type equipment sized for the horsepower of these two tractors included: moldboard and disk plows; disk tillers; disk, spike-tooth and spring-tooth harrows; packer; roller; rotary hoe; corn planter; transplanter; grain drill; mower; rake; manure spreader; hay loader; potato digger and farm wagon. The "L" and "LA" had belt pulley power to run a corn sheller, feed mill, grain elevator, cement mixer, wood saw and small hay press, as shown at right.

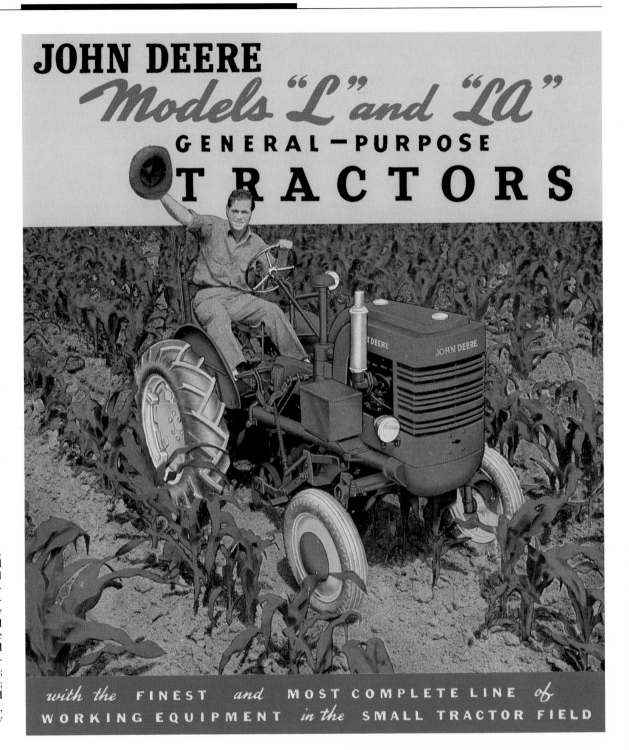

MODEL H

Despite the increasing popularity of tractors, many farmers kept their horses until well through the 1930s. Some plowed and tilled with a tractor, but preferred Old Dobbin for other jobs, especially for the meticulous cultivating. Others, on small farms, felt the size of their operations simply did not justify a tractor. So, horses and mules remained important sources of farm power. But in 1939, when John Deere introduced the Model "H," the days of the draft horse were numbered.

The "H" became the fourth, and smallest-ever, member of the John Deere General Purpose family. Announcement literature reasoned that, ". . . today's farming demands power put up in just the right package to meet most economically, the requirements of each size of farm.

"The farmer who buys too little power either for his jobs or for the size of his farm cannot handle his equipment efficiently nor get his work done in the time he has available. He loses many times over the money he saved in purchasing a smaller tractor than he needed. Likewise, the farmer who buys too much power in a tractor pays a penalty—in first cost, fuel cost, maintenance cost, equipment cost, and depreciation.

"That's why John Deere builds four power sizes in General Purpose tractors—there's one that's just right for handling your jobs efficiently and most economically." When considering the big standard tread "D," the "H" was actually the fifth power size in the John Deere line.

The little "H" met the small farmer's needs for row-crop power at a price he could afford. In addition, he could become even more productive. For example, the 8-acres-per-day capacity of a 1-row horse-drawn cultivator became 25 to 35 with a John Deere "H" and 2-row cultivator.

This little tractor was welcome on large farms as well, as an economical source of auxiliary power on lighter jobs that did not demand all the power offered by the larger, primary tractor.

Built along the same lines of the already widely popular "A" and "B," and the still new to the line "G," the "H" shared most of the features of those larger row-crop tractors. Four variations were produced: "H," "HN," "HWH," and "HNH." The "High" versions offered an outstanding 25 inches of clearance for work in tall-growing vegetables in varying row widths.

In the Nebraska testing laboratory late in 1938, the "H" rated 9.68 drawbar horsepower and 12.97 at the belt pulley. This was the only time this tractor was tested at Nebraska before being replaced in 1947 by the "M."

The always-styled "H" was available only with rubber tires, an all-fuel engine and a 3-speed transmission. Top speeds were 2½ miles per hour in first, 3½ in second, 5¾ in third, and 1¾ in reverse. However, road speed could be increased to 7½ miles per hour using a foot throttle and running the engine at 1800 revolutions per minute.

a Tractor that will Replace *your* Animal Power

The "H" helped break through farmers' natural reluctance to break away from horses and move ahead to tractor power. The page above, from a 1939 sales leaflet, specifically addressed that resistance. The photograph at the right shows an "H" powering a No. 6 Hammermill in 1945. The "H" engine operated at 1400 revolutions per minute, compared with 975 revolutions per minute on the "A." This required a larger "over pulley" to provide proper belt speed for grinding corn and cob meal.

For cultivation, the cleanly designed "H" had a narrow, tapered hood (below) for very good visibility. A complete line of matched working equipment, including cultivators and planters, perfectly suited the "H" for 2-row farming (pictures on far right). The benefits offered with the "H," spelled out on this cutaway from sales materials, were virtually the same as those offered by the three larger General Purpose tractors in the John Deere line in 1940.

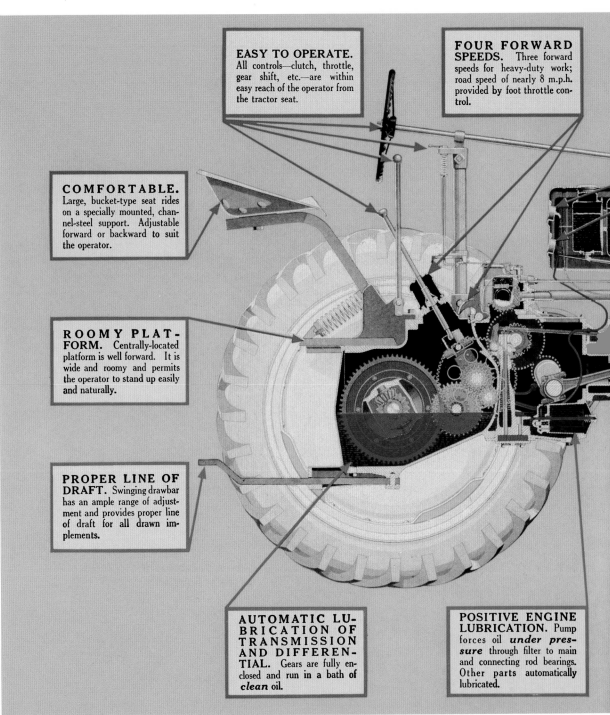

EASY TO OPERATE. All controls—clutch, throttle, gear shift, etc.—are within easy reach of the operator from the tractor seat.

FOUR FORWARD SPEEDS. Three forward speeds for heavy-duty work; road speed of nearly 8 m.p.h. provided by foot throttle control.

COMFORTABLE. Large, bucket-type seat rides on a specially mounted, channel-steel support. Adjustable forward or backward to suit the operator.

ROOMY PLAT-FORM. Centrally-located platform is well forward. It is wide and roomy and permits the operator to stand up easily and naturally.

PROPER LINE OF DRAFT. Swinging drawbar has an ample range of adjustment and provides proper line of draft for all drawn implements.

AUTOMATIC LU-BRICATION OF TRANSMISSION AND DIFFEREN-TIAL. Gears are fully enclosed and run in a bath of *clean* oil.

POSITIVE ENGINE LUBRICATION. Pump forces oil *under pressure* through filter to main and connecting rod bearings. Other parts automatically lubricated.

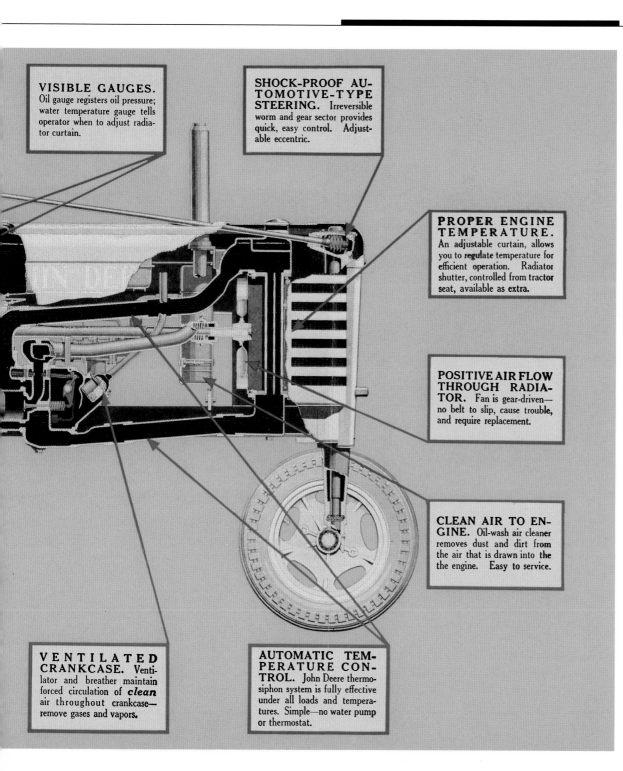

VISIBLE GAUGES. Oil gauge registers oil pressure; water temperature gauge tells operator when to adjust radiator curtain.

SHOCK-PROOF AUTOMOTIVE-TYPE STEERING. Irreversible worm and gear sector provides quick, easy control. Adjustable eccentric.

PROPER ENGINE TEMPERATURE. An adjustable curtain, allows you to regulate temperature for efficient operation. Radiator shutter, controlled from tractor seat, available as extra.

POSITIVE AIR FLOW THROUGH RADIATOR. Fan is gear-driven— no belt to slip, cause trouble, and require replacement.

CLEAN AIR TO ENGINE. Oil-wash air cleaner removes dust and dirt from the air that is drawn into the the engine. Easy to service.

VENTILATED CRANKCASE. Ventilator and breather maintain forced circulation of *clean* air throughout crankcase— remove gases and vapors.

AUTOMATIC TEMPERATURE CONTROL. John Deere thermosiphon system is fully effective under all loads and temperatures. Simple—no water pump or thermostat.

JOHN DEERE SCORES ANOTHER SMASH HIT FOR WESTERN GROWERS

MODEL "HWH" for Bedded Crops

The ideal outfit for the small farm, or to replace the last team of horses on the large farm, was the 1939 advertising description comparing the "H" with its bigger brothers—the "A," "B" and "G." The haying scene below illustrates how the low horsepower "H" could serve on both large and small farms. No one will ever know how many youngsters growing up on farms got their first tractor-driving experience steering for the hay loader.

The early "HN" at the far left shows that the "H" was always styled. The "N" in its name identifies this as an "H" with single front wheel, designed for work in narrow row spacings.

The limited-edition "HWH," a high-clearance and wide front-tread Model "H," was specially built for Western growers. With less than 10 horsepower at the drawbar, this economical-to-operate tractor was perfect for cultivating and harvesting tall plants growing on raised beds.

The "H" is easy to distinguish from its very similar-appearing brothers because it has one stack instead of two. Notice in the raking scene at the far left how only the muffler is upright. The detail below shows how air was drawn in through a screened opening on the left side of the tractor's hood. This is the only model with such an air intake.

Immediate left: The "H" advertising reminded the potential owner that, "The integral equipment you can get for your tractor is as important as the tractor itself." Thus, John Deere offered a complete line of matched equipment—drawn, integral, belt and power-driven—to go with each tractor in the company's line.

MODEL M

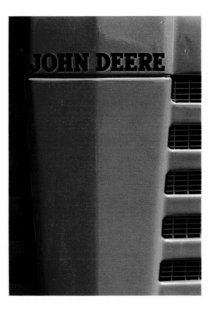

With the end of World War II, John Deere turned its attention to the power needs of nearly 4 million North American farmers who farmed fewer than 100 acres. Typically, these farmers still relied on horses, mules, used or home-made tractors. John Deere also realized that there was a growing need for a second, smaller tractor on many large-acreage farms or on farms with a sizable livestock enterprise.

The early developmental work on a new small tractor took place at both the John Deere Wagon Works in Moline, Illinois, where the "L" and "LA" Tractors were still being built, and at the Waterloo (Iowa) Tractor Company, where the Model "H" Tractor was still in production. However, when the new tractor design was near finalization, neither of these factories were given the task to manufacture it. Instead, the assignment went to a new factory specifically built for the job: the John Deere Dubuque (Iowa) Tractor Company.

This new small tractor was the John Deere Model "M" General Purpose Utility Tractor. It was introduced in 1946, went into full production in 1947, and stayed in the line until 1952.

The Model "M" was called a 1-2-plow tractor, because it could pull one 16-inch bottom or two 12- or 14-inch bottoms, depending on soil conditions. With a vertical, 2-cylinder, valve-in-head engine, this tractor was rated at 14 horsepower at the drawbar and 18 horsepower at the belt pulley at 1650 revolutions per minute. It was said to have "four square" engine displacement, because the bore and stroke were each 4 inches. The "M," like its ancestors, was a simple, economical tractor to operate and maintain. For its size and weight, it had excellent lugging ability and good dependability.

Advertising literature claimed that the Model "M," "does not merely replace horses or mules, it makes possible an improved method of farming." This claim was based on two new time- and labor-saving features. The first was a Quick-Tatch system that enabled the tractor operator to hook up integral equipment easily without leaving the tractor seat. "So easy, so simple, the farmer can detach the equipment and drive the tractor to the house for lunch."

The second feature was Touch-O-Matic hydraulic control. The "M" provided the operator with hydraulic power to raise, lower or set implements at the desired working depth, replacing the foot-operated mechanical lift or hand-operated levers used previously.

The "M" also provided the operator with several comfort and convenience features, such as an adjustable, air-cushioned, bench-type seat with low, padded backrest. The steering wheel could be slid forward or back 12 inches, enabling the operator to sit or stand comfortably when driving the tractor. Special consideration was given to locating all the controls where the operator could easily reach them. The electric starter, rubber tires and PTO were all standard equipment.

The "M" had four forward speeds. First gear was 1⅝ miles per hour; in second, 3⅛ miles per hour; in third, 4¼ miles per hour; and fourth was a transport speed of up to 12 miles per hour. Reverse speed was 1⅝ miles per hour. Second gear was used primarily for plowing; third for cultivating.

The 1-row picker is a very good example of the Quick-Tatch feature of the Model "M" tractor. This wheel-and-drawbar-mounted picker could be hitched or unhitched in little more time than it took to hook on to a pull-type picker. This was an important sales feature at a time when farmers were used to committing a tractor to a picker for the entire corn harvest season.

With 21 inches of crop clearance and individual rear-wheel brakes, the "M" was a handy tractor for cultivating row crops. The rear-wheel tread was adjustable to 38, 42, 48 or 52 inches. A 40-inch front-wheel tread was standard, but an adjustable front axle was available to provide the same tread settings as the rear wheels.

In 1949, John Deere introduced the "MT" Tractor. It was similar to the "M," except that it was basically a row-crop tractor instead of a utility tractor. While the "M" was considered a 1-row tractor, the "MT" could plant or cultivate two rows. The "MT" was available in a tricycle configuration with either one or two front wheels; or with an adjustable front axle. The rear-wheel tread was adjustable from 48 to 96 inches. The "MT" also had larger diameter rear wheels and tires.

The "MT" had as standard equipment dual Touch-O-Matic hydraulic controls. This system enabled the operator to raise or lower cultivators one side at a time or front and rear tool bars independently. The "MT" stayed in the line until 1952.

In addition to a wide variety of integral equipment for seedbed preparation, planting and cultivating, a new rear-mounted sicklebar mower was available for the "M" and "MT." Also, a 1-row, wheel-and-hitch-mounted corn picker added to the versatility and extended the use season of these two small tractors.

In 1949, John Deere also introduced the "MC" Crawler Tractor. Although today's John Deere industrial crawlers evolved from this "little giant," it initially was thought of as a farm or orchard tractor with 2-3-plow power. The "MC" was designed for the farmer who desired extra flotation or more traction or added stability. Prior to the "MC," these needs were met by attaching a Lindeman crawler undercarriage to a Model "BO" chassis. John Deere bought the Lindeman Manufacturing Company of Yakima, Washington, and moved production to Dubuque, Iowa.

The "MC" had 12-inch crawler tracks as standard equipment; 10- or 14-inch "shoes" were optional.

At right is a Model "M" General Purpose Tractor being test driven at the meeting where it was introduced to John Deere executives and engineers. At far right is an advertisement that introduced the "M" to farmers. Note that the "M" was promoted two ways: the only tractor for small farms, a second tractor for big farms. Also note that the Quick-Tatch and Touch-O-Matic systems were cited as the most significant design features.

Above is the Model "MT" which was introduced in 1949. It was basically a Model "M" in a tricycle configuration with added crop clearance and dual hydraulic controls.

Meet the NEW JOHN DEERE Model "M"

GENERAL PURPOSE TRACTOR

With Complete Line of "QUIK-TATCH" WORKING EQUIPMENT

When you choose a new Model "M" Tractor you choose the key unit for a complete and up-to-the-minute farming system. Here is new simplicity, amazing new ease of attaching and detaching a wide variety of machines that will open your eyes. Only a demonstration by your John Deere dealer can tell the full story. Integral and semi-integral equipment includes plows (moldboard and disk), two-way plow, bedder, lister, planters, fertilizer attachments, cultivators (row-crop and field), mower, manure spreader, corn picker, beet lifter, duster, bean harvester and peanut puller, spring-tooth harrow, and many others. Many horse tools can easily be adapted for use with the Model "M".

The Logical Place to Begin in Planning Your "Farm of Tomorrow"

Don't go on farming the hard way. Plan now to raise your crops—do all your farming jobs—at big savings in time, labor, and money with a John Deere Model "M" Tractor and matched equipment.

To get a quick idea of the power of this John Deere, just imagine a tractor weighing 2700 pounds that will step in and pull a two-bottom 14-inch plow, a two-bottom 12-inch plow, or a one-bottom 16-inch plow, (depending upon soil conditions) or a 6-foot double action disk harrow.

Here is a simple, compact tractor a boy can operate . . . a tractor easy to understand . . . easy to handle.

Its simple, two-cylinder vertical valve-in-head engine has all the latest features, including fuel filter, oil-wash air cleaner, thermo-siphon cooling, high-tension magneto, force-feed lubrication, and crankcase breather.

It is regularly equipped with foot-operated independent rear wheel brakes, adjustable rear wheel tread, rubber tires, electric starter, hydraulic power control system, power-take-off shaft, adjustable air-cushion seat, adjustable steering wheel, and temperature gauge. All control levers and pedals are conveniently located for the operator.

The Model "M" can be furnished with belt pulley if you have belt work to do, and electric lights for night work.

Rear wheels are adjustable for four treads: 38-, 42-, 48-, and 52-inch. Standard tread for the front axle is 40 inches. However, an adjustable axle will be available to give 38-, 42-, 48-, and 52-inch front wheel spacings.

With "TOUCH-O-MATIC" Hydraulic Control

Each Model "M" Tractor is regularly equipped with a built-in hydraulic unit with a simple Touch-o-matic hydraulic control lever. Just a touch of the driver's finger to this handy lever will raise or lower integral tools, and regulate *precisely* the depth at which the tools are to work. The tractor does all the work—no manual effort is required. The unique drawbar on the Model "M" Tractor is the secret of the amazing simplicity John Deere engineers have achieved both in working equipment and its control. The drawbar forms a part of the tractor, the equipment, and the hydraulic control system.

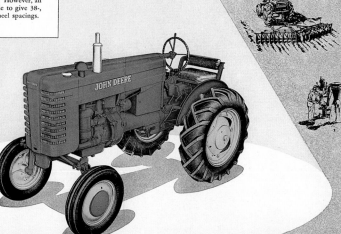

MORE than just a New Tractor - A COMPLETE SYSTEM of FARMING for Smaller Farms...
The ideal, all-around Helper on the Large Farms

The tread width was 36 to 42 inches. Clearance under the chassis was 14 inches. Ground speeds were 1.2 miles per hour in first, 2.2 miles per hour in second, 2.9 miles per hour in third, 6.0 miles per hour in fourth and 1.0 in reverse. Electric starter and PTO were standard; belt pulley and electric lights were extra.

The compact "M" Series Tractors, with their economical performance, hydraulic convenience and easy equipment hookup, were popular with farmers coast to coast. They also were put to use in factories, parks, airports and woodlands, creating an entirely new marketing opportunity for John Deere.

Shown below and at left is the John Deere Dubuque factory as it appeared in the late 1940s when production of the Model "M" Tractor was underway. Located north of Dubuque, Iowa, the factory consisted of 20 major buildings and several smaller structures. It originally had 600,000 square feet of floor space. Many of the men selected to manage the new factory were formerly with the Waterloo, Iowa, John Deere tractor organization. The Dubuque factory is now considerably larger and is dedicated to the design and production of John Deere Industrial Equipment.

JOHN DEERE
Model "MT"
GENERAL-PURPOSE TRACTOR

JOHN DEERE
QUIK-TATCH
WORKING EQUIPMENT

JOHN DEERE
Dual
Touch-o-matic
HYDRAULIC CONTROL

A COMPLETE SYSTEM OF FARMING FOR SMALLER FARMS...IDEAL HELPER ON LARGE FARMS

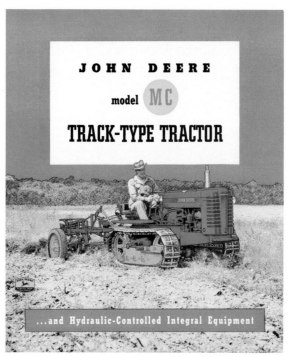

JOHN DEERE
model MC
TRACK-TYPE TRACTOR

...and Hydraulic-Controlled Integral Equipment

The four "M" Series Tractors shown on the opposite page were manufactured at the John Deere Dubuque (Iowa) Tractor Factory during the late 1940s and early 1950s. Starting at right and going counterclockwise, they are: the "M" General Purpose (or "utility") Tractor, shown with a front blade; the "MT" Tricycle or "Row-Crop" Tractor; the "MC" Crawler with dozer blade; the "MI" Industrial Tractor painted Nebraska Orange for highway maintenance work.

Above are covers of early sales folders for the "MT" and "MC" Tractors. The "MC" was originally introduced as a track-type farm tractor, "for use wherever extra flotation is needed." Landscapers and contractors soon put the "MC" to use in industrial applications.

MODEL R

For well over two decades, the "D" carried the load in rice and wheat country. By the mid-40s, of course, the "D" had been refined considerably and its horsepower increased substantially. But just as row-crop farms had grown in acreage, so had wheatland spreads. They demanded "standard" (fixed wheel tread) tractors with still more power. Coincidentally, diesel fuel was becoming increasingly popular in some industrial applications. But adapting diesel engines to agricultural uses posed new technological challenges.

In fact, developing the "R" Diesel represented the largest single engineering task Deere & Company had undertaken up to that time. It involved 66,000 hours of field testing on 16 prototype tractors.

The beginning of the "R" can be traced to the early fall of 1935, a time when very little was known about using diesel engines in wheel-type tractors. But John Deere engineers had already recognized the long-range potential for diesel power and began working intensely to solve the problems. (Beginning in 1972, all John Deere farm tractors had diesel engines.)

Finding a satisfactory means of starting in cold weather was one of the first objectives. Obviously, farm tractors have to be operated in cold, even below freezing, weather. But getting diesels started was difficult.

To understand why, consider the difference between gasoline and diesel-burning engines. In a spark-ignition engine (gasoline, for example), a mixture of fuel and air is drawn into the combustion chamber where it's compressed and ignited by a spark from the spark plug. However, on the intake stroke of a diesel, only air is drawn in. During compression, the air reaches about 1000 degrees Fahrenheit. At this point, diesel fuel is injected into the combustion chamber and the hot air ignites it.

In order to fire the diesel engine in cold weather, warming the combustion chamber becomes necessary. Early 24-volt electrical systems proved too bulky and expensive. However, using a separate gasoline starting engine proved satisfactory, because the exhaust heat from this tiny engine warmed the big diesel engine. Interestingly, this little 24.6 cubic-inch-displacement engine also had two cylinders.

But, the "R" brought more than diesel power to John Deere tractors. It also introduced "live" power takeoff, which permitted engaging or disengaging the PTO independently of the forward motion of the tractor. The first John Deere all-steel cab was available on the "R," too.

Powr-Trol hydraulics was another advancement available to owners of the "R." With this feature, the operator could regulate the working depth of drawn tools, raise or lower plow bottoms and tiller disks, angle or straighten disk harrow gangs . . . all whether the tractor was "on the go" or standing still. Using a lever near his seat, the operator could instantly control a double-acting remote hydraulic cylinder to move the implement as desired. This eliminated the chore of tugging on ropes, reaching for stubborn lifting levers, and raising or lowering heavy equipment by hand.

The "R" was introduced in 1948 for the 1949 model year and stayed in the line through 1954.

Fuel is the single biggest expense of operating a tractor, and the fuel economy of the Model "R" diesel was phenomenal for its time. These big tractors were used mainly in the vast Western plains, so they could easily save owners several hundred dollars a year on fuel.

JOHN DEERE
Model "R"
DIESEL

THE COST-REDUCING TRACTOR

they're all talking about

JOHN DEERE
QUALITY FARM
EQUIPMENT

This new tractor "looks powerful and it is powerful, it looks modern and it is modern" read the advertising announcing the "entirely new, not remodeled" Model "R." The text went on: "A heavyweight among wheel-type tractors, the "R" has a knockout punch to whip those tough jobs . . . the speed to work heavy-duty equipment at maximum capacity and cut days off your working calendar . . . the stamina to slug it out continuously in hard, grueling conditions with fewer timeouts for adjustment and repair." Below: The "R" was equipped with a 5-speed transmission. Bottom: Several-step fuel filtering was required to prevent particles as small as 0.0001 inch in diameter from clogging the diesel injectors.

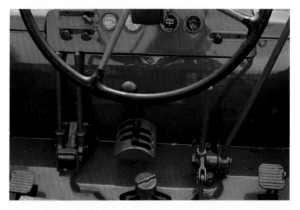

With its 34 drawbar horsepower, the "R" could easily pull tandem-hitched drills heavily loaded with seed. The wide, cushioned, adjustable seat shown below permitted the operator to work in comfort, high above dust and dirt. Bottom: The oscillating front axle cushioned shocks and provided flexibility when working on rough ground. This handy front hitch proved useful in all kinds of situations, such as pushing implements into storage or keeping the tractor's rear drive wheels on solid footing while pulling equipment out of the mud.

I n 1952, for the first time, John Deere began the planned introduction of a tractor "family." Admittedly, toward the end of their stay in the line, the lettered models greatly resembled each other style- and features-wise. But this had come about over nearly a 30-year period . . . the "D" was introduced in 1923, the "A" in 1934, the "B" in 1935, the "L" in 1937, the "G"in 1938, the "H" in 1939, the "LA" in 1941, the "M" in 1947 (which replaced the "L," "H" and "LA"), and the "MT" and "R" in 1949. Significant styling changes had also occurred during this span, however, not all at once. For a period during World War II, for example, the "A," "B" and "H" were styled while the biggest member of the four General Purpose models (the "G") was not.

Certainly, this was an evolutionary time in tractor development. New models were added to the line as the market needs arose and as the rapidly escalating technological advances so dictated.

But by the early 1950s, tractor configurations had been pretty much established and the rampant advances in "basic" technology had slowed. It became time for planned coordination when introducing new models. For sure, this philosophical change in manufacturing and marketing strategy couldn't be made all at once. But, its time had arrived . . . and the "First Numbered Series" was born.

Within a three-year period, five new models were flowing off the assembly lines in Waterloo and Dubuque. Despite being built at two different factories in Iowa, these new models shared more in common than had the seven earlier models which they replaced. Each offered more horsepower plus significant performance and convenience refinements as compared with its predecessor.

For example, the Numbered models offered exclusive duplex carburetion. Essentially, this involved a 2-barrel carburetor, which fed identical amounts of fuel and air to each cylinder. According to the advertising literature this resulted in "faster starts, snappier response, smoother operation at all throttle

---

This 1957 photo illustrates how both tractor technology and equipment had advanced in the 34 years since the John Deere "D" was first built. "Live" PTO and high-pressure hydraulics could completely take over the hand work of putting hay on the wagon. Above: With optional power steering, maneuvering increasingly larger and more powerful tractors became finger easy.

settings, outstanding fuel economy and prolonged spark plug life."

Another refinement also helped make the exclusive John Deere 2-cylinder powerplants "today's most modern, most time-proved tractor engines." An "eyebrow" over each intake valve caused a swirling turbulence which more thoroughly mixed the fuel and air going into the cylinders. Called "Cyclonic Fuel Intake," this resulted in better combustion and, therefore, greater operating economy.

Thanks to "All-Weather" manifolds these engines offered excellent fuel efficiency in both summer and winter. Through the use of a 2-position valve, exhaust gases could be directed around or away from the fuel/air passageways. Thus, in summer the operator

could use a cooler mixture and in winter a warmer mixture. During cold weather, such a preheated charge of fuel and air provided more efficient vaporization and more complete combustion.

Additional fuel options became available for the 50, 60, and 70, too. Besides gasoline and "all fuel" engines, they could be equipped with liquified petroleum (LP) engines. Near refineries LP gas could be purchased for as little as 5 cents per gallon, making it economical even though the LP engine cost

slightly more initially and a gallon of clean burning LP wouldn't produce quite as much work as a gallon of gasoline. Although LP must be handled with pressurized equipment, some farmers found this a significant advantage over gasoline . . . which was vulnerable to thieves using siphon tubes.

Although not available initially, the 70 offered a diesel option (the first John Deere diesel for row-crop farmers). In its Nebraska test, the 70 diesel set a new fuel-economy record, bettering all previously tested row-crop tractors. A year later, when the 80 diesel was tested, it set the all-time record for diesel fuel economy up to that point.

The Numbered tractors also brought significant improvements in operator convenience. An adjustable backrest on the seat, and longer hand clutch and throttle levers put these controls within easier reach of the operator. Changing rear wheel spacing was greatly simplified, thanks to another industry first . . . rack-and-pinion rear tread adjustment.

In 1954, the 50, 60 and 70 became the first row-crop tractors equipped with optional factory-installed power steering. It became standard equipment during their lifetimes. John Deere engineers achieved this industry first with a system that used built-in hydaulics to control the steering column. This advancement differed from "add-on" systems utilizing externally mounted motors on steering shafts or hydraulic cylinders hooked up to tie rods.

"Every time you take the wheel, tireless hydraulic muscles save you time and work. You'll marvel how easily the tractor handles—through deep sand or mud . . . in bedded or irrigated land . . . over rough ground—in extreme as well as in average conditions. And, your wife, son, daughter, or an older member of the family can handle the tractor just as easily, just as surely as you, yourself," read the promotional materials of the day.

Modernization in equipment control paralleled improvements in tractor power and performance, too. A "live" powershaft provided continuous power for operating PTO-driven equipment. "Live" high-pressure Powr-Trol hydraulics provided increased muscle to handle heavier drawn and integral implements. Dual Touch-O-Matic hydraulic control permitted independent or coordinated raising and lowering of front- and rear-mounted cultivator gangs or other implements.

ere are all five models in the First Numbered Series, including some of the various configurations available. From left to right: the general purpose 34-hp 70 diesel, the 46-hp 80 with optional cab, the 27-hp 60 Orchard, the 20-hp 50, and the 17-hp 40 Utility. Not all models were introduced at the same time . . . the 50 and 60 came first, in 1952 (except for the 60 Orchard which wasn't built until 1953) . . . the 40 and 70 became available in 1953 . . . and the 80 was introduced last, in 1955.

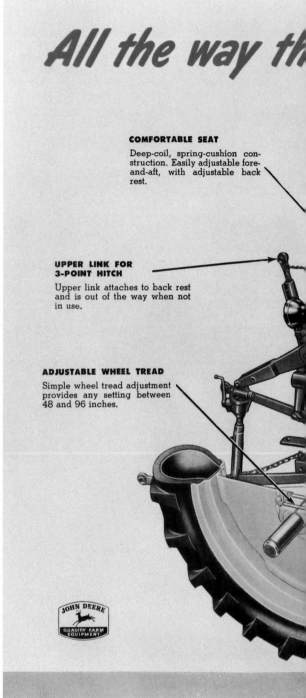

The name "Utility" applied to the version of the 40 appearing on this page. This well-chosen description expressed the tractor's wide range of usefulness wherever ground-hugging stability and quick maneuverability were needed. Orchardists, citrus growers, vineyardists, hay growers, hops growers, and many general farmers chose this version. However, for other applications the 40 was available as a crawler and in general-purpose styles (single front wheel, tricycle with dual front wheels, or wide front end), Special, Hi-Crop and crawler versions also. As these 1953 advertising pages promised, the 40 proved a wise choice no matter which style the user selected.

ough...the Model "40" is a truly great tractor

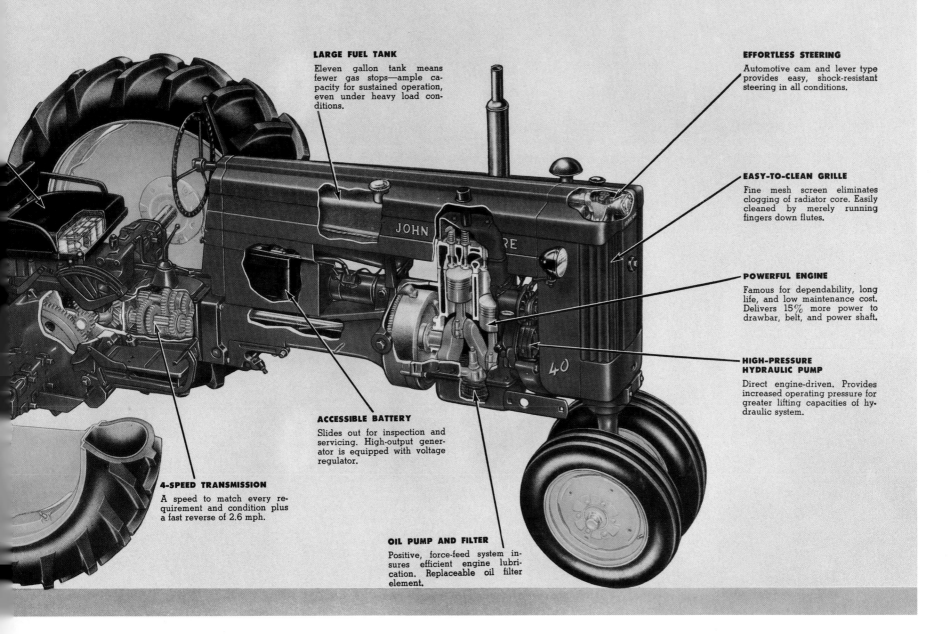

LARGE FUEL TANK

Eleven gallon tank means fewer gas stops—ample capacity for sustained operation, even under heavy load conditions.

EFFORTLESS STEERING

Automotive cam and lever type provides easy, shock-resistant steering in all conditions.

EASY-TO-CLEAN GRILLE

Fine mesh screen eliminates clogging of radiator core. Easily cleaned by merely running fingers down flutes.

POWERFUL ENGINE

Famous for dependability, long life, and low maintenance cost. Delivers 15% more power to drawbar, belt, and power shaft.

HIGH-PRESSURE HYDRAULIC PUMP

Direct engine-driven. Provides increased operating pressure for greater lifting capacities of hydraulic system.

ACCESSIBLE BATTERY

Slides out for inspection and servicing. High-output generator is equipped with voltage regulator.

4-SPEED TRANSMISSION

A speed to match every requirement and condition plus a fast reverse of 2.6 mph.

OIL PUMP AND FILTER

Positive, force-feed system insures efficient engine lubrication. Replaceable oil filter element.

They're Newcomers with a Pedigree

MEET THE John Deere "50" and "60" Tractors—the brilliant new successors to the famous John Deere Models "B" and "A."

These heavy-duty, two- and three-plow tractors offer you many new operating advantages that will save time and speed up every power job on your farm... that will save work and make your farming easier than ever before... that will greatly increase the operating efficiency of your equipment and boost profits.

The Models "50" and "60" are newcomers with a pedigree of almost thirty years' experience in building more than a million farm tractors. In addition to their many new engineering advancements and major improvements shown on the following pages, they offer you all the time-tested, field-proved advantages of exclusive John Deere *two-cylinder* engine design. They're blue-ribbon, quality-built tractors through and through.

THE HEAVY-DUTY 2-PLOW **50**

THE HEAVY-DUTY 3-PLOW **60**

...*featuring* Duplex Carburetion . . . "Live" Power Shaft . . . "Live," High-Pressure Hydraulic Powr-Trol . . . Quick-Change Wheel-Tread . . . Effortless Steering, and many other <u>new</u> features and major engineering improvements

The 1952 introductory sales folder, pages 2 and 3 reproduced above, clearly reveals the Company strategy of comparing these new models with their well-accepted predecessors. After all, with over a half million "A's" and "B's" still serving on farms in the U.S. and Canada, why let prospects feel anything but what the new 50 and 60 were improved "A's" and "B's"? Which, in fact, they were. At left, the elegant lines of a restored 50 deserve to be admired in an appropriate pastoral setting.

While manufacture of the General Purpose 60 began in April of 1952, Standard and Orchard versions didn't appear until the next fall. Visually, the 60 Orchard (far left) looked very much like the late-styled "AO."

At the immediate left, notice how instrumentation had leaped forward. The new, large speed-hour meter in the center of the instrument panel, for example, took much of the guesswork out of tractor operation. It showed engine revolutions per minute, travel speed in all gears, powershaft speed, and the accumulated hours of service.

Below, the 40 Crawler was advertised as "a little giant in power" weighing only 4125 pounds for the four-roller model and 4560 pounds for the five-roller . . . and delivering approximately 15 horsepower at the drawbar.

THE Lightweight CRAWLER

WITH A HEAVYWEIGHT PUNCH

High-pressure Powr-Trol hydaulics came to the Numbered models. Pioneered on John Deere tractors, this was the first dual hydraulic system that was adaptable to virtually all integral and drawn tools. Although introduced in 1945, work capability increased significantly with these new Numbered models. For example, working pressure increased 114 percent on the Model 50 as compared with the "B," rockshaft capacity of the 60 grew by 35 percent over the "A."

Promotional materials indicated that "live" Powr-Trol hydaulics "saves up to 40 percent of the time and effort formerly required in clutching and shifting gears when operating manure loaders . . . in hooking or unhooking tool carrier attachments . . . or whenever the tractor travel must be stopped and the equipment operated by hydaulic power."

The top photo on this page shows the hydraulic control lever, located just to the right of the seat. The picture at the bottom left shows the crank for raising and lowering one of the lower arms of the 3-point hitch. This permitted aligning the hitch for hooking up to implements and for releveling the hitch for correct operation.

Bottom right: In 1955, this exclamation announced diesel power in a second-size John Deere tractor. Prior to this, the 80 and the "R" which it replaced were the only John Deere diesels. Pictured on the next page is the Model 70 Standard Tractor. This was a somewhat unusual "Standard" tractor, in that it was a wheatland tractor built on a row-crop chassis. Only the fenders and front axle distinguished the two versions.

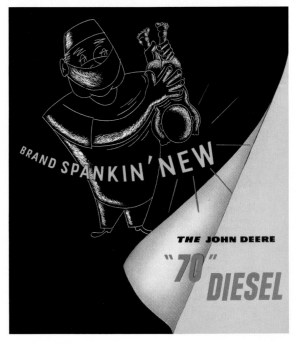

BRAND SPANKIN' NEW

THE JOHN DEERE

"70" DIESEL

The 80, pictured at the far right, completed the First Numbered line. This big diesel tractor replaced the "R" and was officially rated at 46 drawbar horsepower, slightly over half again as much as its predecessor.

Also, with its new 6-speed transmission (below), the 80 provided the brawn and gearing to pull a 5-bottom plow, handle 21 feet of double-action disk harrow, and pull double hookups of hydraulically controlled field cultivators, tool carriers, rod weeders and grain drills in a wide range of conditions.

Right: Welcome on tall 50s, 60s and 70s, this rear exhaust muffler could be field installed to afford maximum clearance when working under low sheds and doorways. This arrangement carried exhaust fumes and noise to the rear and discharged them away from the operator. Since the air intake was already under the hood, adding this special rear exhaust left a clean, unobstructed view over the top of the hood.

20 SERIES

Although John Deere began introducing a full line of tractors in 1952, it still took three years to bring in all five "Numbered" models. By 1956, the continuing advancements in tractor design, plus engine refinements which boosted horsepower outputs, justified another change in model designations. However, this time, the entire line was replaced all at once. In fact, not only did the 40 become the 420, the 50 the 520, the 60 the 620, the 70 the 720, and the 80 the 820, but also a new smaller size, the 320, was added. "Power sizes and types to meet every farming need," read the advertising literature announcing the "six power sizes . . . 30 basic models."

Two big differences stood out between the "old" and the "new"—new styling which was immediately visible, and more power which wasn't noticeable until the new models and those they replaced were operated side by side. The 18 to 25 percent increases in horsepower of the 420 through 720 were then also immediately visible.

Initially, the 820 had the same engine and same power as the 80, but later on new pistons and fuel-injection changes raised its muscle by more than 12 percent and it became the first John Deere tractor with more than 50 drawbar horsepower.

Incidentally, horsepower figures referred to throughout this book are taken from the published results of the Tractor Tests conducted by the Nebraska testing laboratory. In order for tractors to be sold in Nebraska, their horsepowers and other performance characteristics must be verified by the state's Department of Agriculture. Since a "neutral" party conducts these tests, and the procedures compare all tractors exactly the same way, the results can be regarded as "official."

However, the Nebraska Tests report figures in three ways: "Observed," "Corrected" mathematically to reflect a standard condition (60 degrees F. and sea level barometric pressure), and "Rated." We've quoted the rated figures because they most closely reflect power available in average tractor working conditions. However, they appear as lower figures because they're the "corrected" drawbar scores multiplied by 0.75 (or the belt horsepower times 0.85).

Using the "rated" drawbar horsepowers, then, here's a size comparison of models in this new line: 20-hp 420, 26-hp 520, 33-hp 620, 40-hp 720, and 52-hp 820. (The 320 was not tested in Nebraska.)

But more powerful engines were just one of the many advantages of owning a "20" Series Tractor. For example, Load-and-Depth Control helped keep implements working at a uniform depth. When needed, weight was automatically transferred to the tractor drive wheels to maintain traction. In extremely tough conditions, the system raised the implement just enough to relieve the load and allow the tractor to move ahead steadily. When working through depressions or over ridges, the system automatically compensated to maintain the uniform working depth.

The "20s" introduced new operator comfort, too. An optional Float-Ride Seat on the larger models, supported on rubber torsion springs could be adjusted accurately to each operator's weight. This seat was also adjustable forward and back to fit the operator's height and reach.

Reading from the 420 sales folder, here was an-

Custom Powr-Trol hydraulics came with the restyled 720 (closeup above) and all models in the new line. In the field (left), this advanced hydraulic system offered both fast and slow speeds for raising or lowering equipment; "fast" for raising a disk, for example, on the headlands, "slow" for "inching" equipment up or down to accommodate changing field conditions.

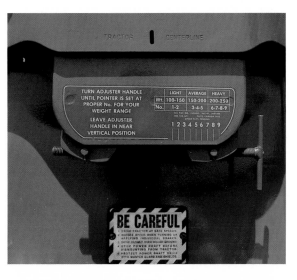

other welcome option: "Where rear-wheel treads must be changed frequently, these special power-adjusted rear wheels will save your time and muscle. Just loosen three clamps and set the handy stop at the spacing desired. Then get on the tractor, ease in the clutch, and presto! . . . engine power slides the rear wheels in or out to the position selected. The wheels are power-spaced from the tractor seat, several times a day if necessary, at the barn or in the field."

Numerous other refinements improved durability and operating convenience throughout the line.

Excerpts from the 1956 advertising folder introducing the 320 adeptly categorize and sell this new size in the John Deere tractor line. "Do you own or operate a small farm? Are you a truck gardener? A large-acreage farmer who needs an auxiliary tractor for the lighter farming jobs?

"If you fall into one of these general classifications, you will want to investigate the thrifty new John Deere 320 Series Tractors because they have been designed and built specifically for you. What's more, these tractors offer you the many advantages of modern John Deere power farming at a price in keeping with your power needs.

"The 320 Standard, with its 21-inch clearance handles all-around farming work, including 1-row planting, fertilizing and cultivating" . . . "ideally adapted for such crops as tobacco, cotton, corn, peanuts, hay, strawberries, and vegetables.

"The 320 Utility is a low-built tractor for field, orchard, grove, and vineyard work, mowing of all kinds, and industrial jobs" . . . "stands only 50 inches high at the hood line, providing unusual stability on uneven ground" . . . "extra-good clearance under tree limbs and low buildings.

"You have power to pull two 12-inch plow bottoms in most soils, to handle a 6-foot double-action disk harrow, or to operate a 7-foot mower.

"Top all this with rock-bottom economy—the dollars and cents savings that make John Deere tractors the true economy leaders—and you will see what we mean when we say your best buy in a 1-2-plow tractor is a John Deere 320."

Besides the above, "striking handsomeness" might have been added . . . as revealed by the full-page portrait and decal close-up of the 320 Utility. Lower left photo: The "1-2 plow" description referred to capability for pulling "2-12s" (two 12-inch plow bottoms) in normal conditions or "1-16" (one 16-inch bottom) in tough going, such as heavy clay soils.

Above, immediate left: Predictably, the features farmers admired in large tractors were the same ones they asked for in smaller models, such as adjustable seats to match the weight of the operator.

The 420 equipped with dual-wheel tricycle front-end, pictured at the left, appeared visually to be a little brother of the 520, 620 and 720. Comparing the features spelled out on the 420 cutaway below with those of the bigger row-crop models proved that, indeed, these four tractors belonged in the same family. The 20-hp 420 came in several other configurations, too . . . General Purpose versions with wide front wheels or single front wheel, Hi-Crop with 32 inches of under-axle clearance, Special with 26-inch clearance over the row and a wide range of wheel spacings, Standard for one-row cultivating, and two Utility models (one for orchard/vineyard work and the other for straddling and cultivating two rows).

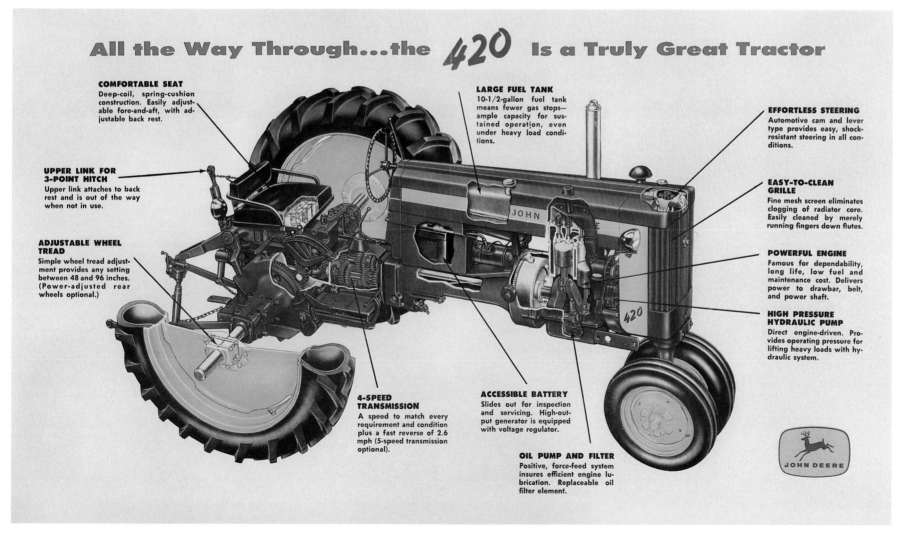

All the Way Through...the 420 Is a Truly Great Tractor

COMFORTABLE SEAT
Deep-coil, spring-cushion construction. Easily adjustable fore-and-aft, with adjustable back rest.

UPPER LINK FOR 3-POINT HITCH
Upper link attaches to back rest and is out of the way when not in use.

ADJUSTABLE WHEEL TREAD
Simple wheel tread adjustment provides any setting between 48 and 96 inches. (Power-adjusted rear wheels optional.)

4-SPEED TRANSMISSION
A speed to match every requirement and condition plus a fast reverse of 2.6 mph (5-speed transmission optional).

LARGE FUEL TANK
10-1/2-gallon fuel tank means fewer gas stops—ample capacity for sustained operation, even under heavy load conditions.

ACCESSIBLE BATTERY
Slides out for inspection and servicing. High-output generator is equipped with voltage regulator.

OIL PUMP AND FILTER
Positive, force-feed system insures efficient engine lubrication. Replaceable oil filter element.

EFFORTLESS STEERING
Automotive cam and lever type provides easy, shock-resistant steering in all conditions.

EASY-TO-CLEAN GRILLE
Fine mesh screen eliminates clogging of radiator core. Easily cleaned by merely running fingers down flutes.

POWERFUL ENGINE
Famous for dependability, long life, low fuel and maintenance cost. Delivers power to drawbar, belt, and power shaft.

HIGH PRESSURE HYDRAULIC PUMP
Direct engine-driven. Provides operating pressure for lifting heavy loads with hydraulic system.

JOHN DEERE

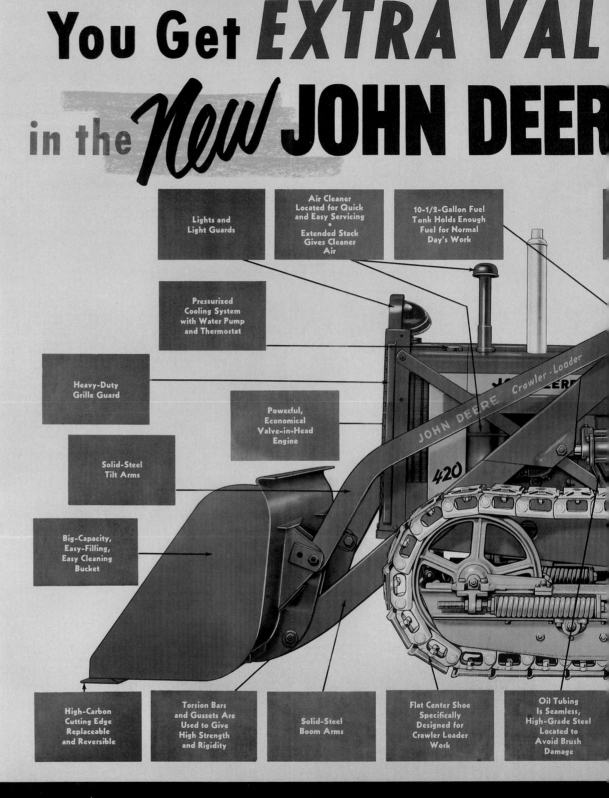

You Get EXTRA VAL
in the *New* JOHN DEER

Lights and Light Guards

Air Cleaner Located for Quick and Easy Servicing • Extended Stack Gives Cleaner Air

10-1/2-Gallon Fuel Tank Holds Enough Fuel for Normal Day's Work

Pressurized Cooling System with Water Pump and Thermostat

Heavy-Duty Grille Guard

Powerful, Economical Valve-in-Head Engine

Solid-Steel Tilt Arms

Big-Capacity, Easy-Filling, Easy Cleaning Bucket

High-Carbon Cutting Edge Replaceable and Reversible

Torsion Bars and Gussets Are Used to Give High Strength and Rigidity

Solid-Steel Boom Arms

Flat Center Shoe Specifically Designed for Crawler Loader Work

Oil Tubing Is Seamless, High-Grade Steel Located to Avoid Brush Damage

JOHN DEERE Crawler-Loader

420

▶ See This Remarkable Unit a

E from Stem to Stern
CRAWLER LOADER

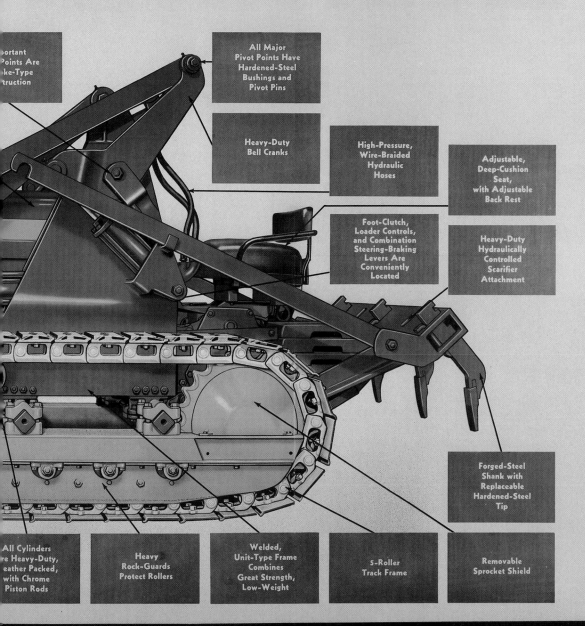

portant
Points Are
ke-Type
truction

All Major
Pivot Points Have
Hardened-Steel
Bushings and
Pivot Pins

Heavy-Duty
Bell Cranks

High-Pressure,
Wire-Braided
Hydraulic
Hoses

Adjustable,
Deep-Cushion
Seat,
with Adjustable
Back Rest

Foot-Clutch,
Loader Controls,
and Combination
Steering-Braking
Levers Are
Conveniently
Located

Heavy-Duty
Hydraulically
Controlled
Scarifier
Attachment

Forged-Steel
Shank with
Replaceable
Hardened-Steel
Tip

All Cylinders
re Heavy-Duty,
eather Packed,
with Chrome
Piston Rods

Heavy
Rock-Guards
Protect Rollers

Welded,
Unit-Type Frame
Combines
Great Strength,
Low-Weight

5-Roller
Track Frame

Removable
Sprocket Shield

Pacific Northwest orchardists pioneered the use of small crawlers because these tractors provided hillside stability. Soon though, the good flotation of little crawlers appealed to New England maple sugar producers who tended their trees while snow still covered the ground, to Southern foresters who cut timber in swampy woodlands, to builders who needed a tractor to scoot over mounds of freshly excavated soil, and to farmers who needed to work in fields too wet and soggy to support wheeled tractors.

Tailoring a crawler for industrial work, even for "light" construction and utility applications, required significant beefing up over what was needed for pulling a plow on farmland. The 420 could be equipped with an economical 4-roller track system or, as shown, with five rollers for maximum flotation, traction, and fore-and-aft stability.

Far left, crawler owners considered radiator shields an absolute necessity in woodlot, orchard, and forest operations to protect the radiator and lights from branches.

In the photo below, notice how yellow paint began to dress up even more the attractive design ushered in on the First Numbered tractors. At right, whichever model of tractor the farmer chose, he could select from a complete line of John Deere implements matched precisely to his tractor's power and to the soil conditions.

Below left, the 20 Series introduced Custom Powr-Trol hydraulics, which enabled the operator to set working depth precisely. After raising the implements and turning at the end of the field, an adjustable stop let the operator return the tool to the preset depth.

If the 620 Orchard Tractor pictured at right reminds you of the late-styled "AO" and the 60 covered in earlier chapters, you're right. Beneath the sheet metal, there's 26 percent more horsepower and many refinements, but this is basically the same tractor as the "AO." The 620 Orchard Tractor was the last 2-cylinder orchard model.

The General Purpose 620 below illustrates how PTO power was eliminating pulley/belt power. Pulling the "threshing unit" through the field accomplished in one trip what otherwise required cutting the grain with a binder, hand shocking, loading bundles onto wagons by hand, then hauling them to a threshing machine where they had to be pitched into the feeder by hand. Ever thought about the origin of the name "combine"?

Far right: In the 1950s, the greater stability provided by wide-spread front tires on increasingly bigger row-crop tractors began overtaking the tricycle front-ends common since the "GP" Wide-Tread era began in 1929. Typical of the updating farmers make on their still working 2-cylinder tractors, the "30 Series" fenders with dual headlights have been added to this beautifully restored 720.

Page 132-133: All across North America the 620 proved a popular successor to the "A" lineage. This picture shows a uniformed company salesman demonstrating John Deere's new Bale Ejector at a "One-Man Hay Day" near Roanoke, Virginia.

30 SERIES

One more line of new models completed the "Johnny Popper" era. The year was 1958, when John Deere replaced the 320 through 820 with the 330 through 830. After the broad range of performance improvements that had already been incorporated into the First Numbered and 20 Series models, advancements in the new 30 Series Tractors concentrated on operator comfort and convenience. However, these models also received a visually healthy dose of aesthetic refinement. Setting aside any personal loyalties and affections toward certain individual models of 2-cylinder tractors, you'll probably agree that the 330, 430, 530, 630, 730 and 830 together form a most-fitting climax to this unique era. (Turn to pages 148-149 to view just such a lineup.)

The 1958 advertising literature summarized the improvements brought to row-crop farmers by the General-Purpose 30s: "These new tractors are easier to mount, easier to start, easier to shift, quieter to the ear. You'll be able to read the instrument panel more easily, steer from a more natural position, and operate the brakes with new ease and convenience.

New, styled rear fenders provide greater protection from dirt, dust, and mud—from accidental contact with the rear wheels. At night, you'll travel the road or work your fields with a brand-new lighting system that is unique in farm tractors."

Of course, they retained all of the lugging power and operating efficiency for which John Deere numbered tractors had become famous. Although horsepowers didn't change, improved camshaft lubrication and more durable piston rings helped further stretch engine life of these six tractors.

Actually, the 30 Series "family" included one additional member. It was the 435, introduced a year after the others. This was the first John Deere tractor available with 540- and 1000-rpm PTO and industry-standardized PTO specifications. These standards specified dimensions, for example, for size and location of drawbar hitching holes . . . for distances between hitching points and PTO shafts . . . and for safety shielding. Prior to this, attaching points and PTO shafts were not always consistent from manufacturer to manufacturer, making some equipment incompatible with some tractors.

In addition, tractor power and torque were increasing beyond that which could be effectively transmitted through a 540-rpm PTO—the 540 revolutions per minute had been established as an industry standard 35 years earlier, in 1923. Thus, an additional 1000 revolutions per minute PTO standard was established, to increase power-transmitting capacity.

A "New Generation" of higher-horsepower-to-weight 4- and 6-cylinder tractors replaced the 30 Series in 1960 . . . and after four decades, the John Deere Two-Cylinder Era concluded. The time had come, in the United States and Canada at least, when it was no longer practical to continue increasing the physical size of tractors enough to accommodate the higher horsepowers that farming would demand in the rest of the 20th century.

But the two-cylinder days hadn't yet ended, totally. Some 730s were built at Waterloo until early 1961 for export overseas. And many additional 730s were manufactured in Argentina throughout the 1960s . . . perhaps because there were still some horses to be replaced on farms there?

A bigger splash of yellow on newly angled side shielding and hoods, a completely enclosed steering shaft, and new dual-headlight fenders, gave an appealing cosmetic uplift to the 530 and its siblings. At right: One of the many farmer-approved features the 530 inherited was Power-Adjusted rear wheels. This John Deere exclusive (also available on the 430, 435, 630 and 730) made it easy to widen the wheel treads so the operator could run the rear tires between swathes when raking hay and, just as quickly, readjust them for cultivating corn.

Modern FENDERS
with *dual* HEADLIGHTS

Protective fenders shield you from mud, dust, and dirt; provide a convenient handhold for mounting, and carry the modern, unique John Deere dual lighting system. These heavy-duty fenders can be adjusted up or down for various size tires or when chains are used; a two-position lateral adjustment provides greater clearance between tires and fenders. Each fender carries two powerful sealed-beam lights. The inner lights project beams ahead of the tractor; the outer lights flood front-mounted equipment and the work area. The 6-row cultivating operation above shows the excellent illumination these lights provide at night. These fenders and dual lights are available as extra equipment on all "730" General-Purpose Tractors.

The dual front lights are controlled by a single ignition-light switch. On the road, both lights are used in the "bright" position; the inner lights go out when the switch is turned to "dim" to meet oncoming traffic. Sealed beam construction insures longer service; a brilliant beam is provided for the life of the light. Both sets of lights can be easily adjusted.

The 730 diesel at the far left, plowing under wheat stubble in Kansas five furrows at a crack, brought pushbutton electric starting to John Deere tractors with diesel engines. Electric starting was a simpler and less expensive alternative to starting with small, auxiliary gasoline engines. This 730 Standard is equipped with adjustable wheel tread, but it was available also with fixed-tread front and rear axles. New 530, 630 and 730 General Purpose versions could be equipped with row-crop fenders with dual headlights. One light on each side projected a powerful beam forward, while the other flooded the working area of a 6-row cultivator.

As were its 420 and 40 predecessors, the 430 was offered in several different versions. Perhaps the most unusual was the grasshopper-like Hi-Crop model at the far right. Since this particular tractor is equipped with an LP-gas engine (identifiable by the large, rounded fuel tank between the muffler and steering wheel), it is quite rare. But, perhaps not as rare as a 430 Hi-Crop with all-fuel engine. The 630 and 730 were also available in Hi-Crop configurations. Right: The 430 Crawler came in two versions, as illustrated with 5-roller tracks and with lower-cost 4-roller tracks. Below: Shown in northwestern Illinois cutting and conditioning hay in one pass, the 430 Row-Crop Utility Tractor provided handy supplementary power on many medium and large farms. On smaller farms, it was capable of handling all the work.

JOHN DEERE 530 630 730 General-Purpose TRACTORS

Modern power for medium or large-acreage row-crop farms

The two 630s on these two pages illustrate clearly the differences between tractors designed for work in wide-open spaces and those for row-crop farming in more-confined areas.

The 630 Standard, at far left, was described in 1959 advertising literature as being "ideal for medium- and large-acreage grain and rice operations. Its modern, functional styling features a short, compact design; wide rear fenders and a husky, oscillating front axle. Easy-to-operate controls are conveniently located within easy reach." This 630 is equipped with an LP-gas engine.

The 630 Tricycle pictured on the front of the General Purpose brochure, at the immediate left, offered greater crop clearance plus nimbleness for sharp turns at field ends and work in tight quarters. Besides the conventional and Roll-O-Matic dual front-wheel options, the 630 could be equipped with a single front wheel or 48- to 80-inch adjustable, wide front axle. A Hi-Crop version of the 630 was also available.

Horsepowers of the 30 Series models remained the same as those of their 20 Series counterparts. But when farmers stepped up to the improved operator control and comfort on these refined tractors, they could get more work done each day. The 6-plow 830, far right, topped the list size-wise of 2-cylinder John Deere tractors. The oval muffler, new on the 30s, reduced noise levels.

Fender handholds and a step mounted on the rear axle made getting on and off the larger General Purpose, or "row-crop," models easier. Right: A slanted steering wheel, conveniently grouped instruments on lighted panels, and naturally placed controls made operating 30 Series Tractors less fatiguing than earlier models.

Bottom, left to right: Compare the comfort of this adjustable, shock-absorbing seat with the almost-rigid steel seats of early 2-cylinder models. From this "roomy, stand-at-will" platform—protected from Plains-land dirt and riceland mud by the wide fenders—an operator could till up to 100 acres a day with his 830 pulling a 20-foot Surflex tiller. Advertising termed the 830 "Mr. Mighty—a powerful tractor which will inspire the use of larger equipment, more cropland acres, the accomplishment of more work by one man—a man who becomes a Giant in terms of daily work output."

STEP UP to new farming <u>ease</u> and <u>convenience</u>

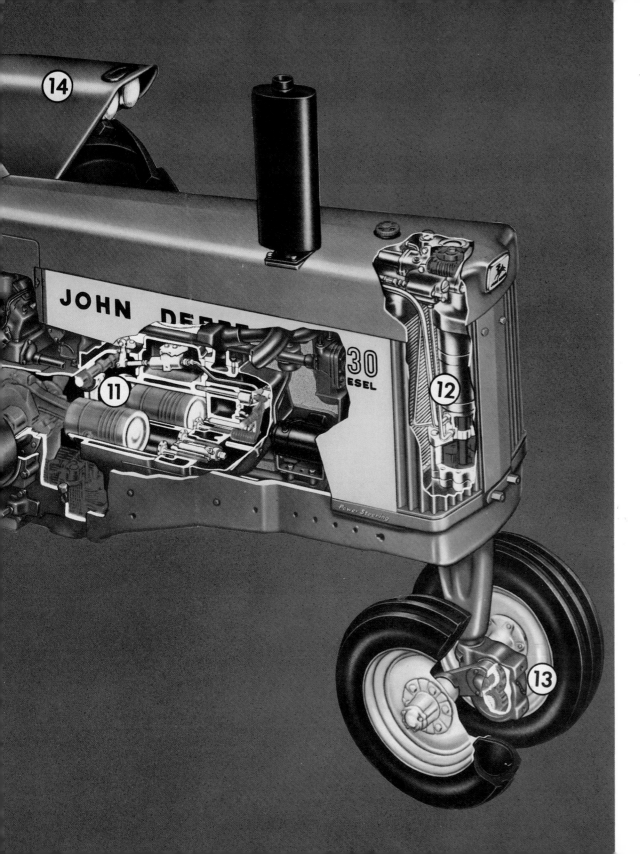

Underneath attractive new styling, explained the advertising, 30 Series Tractors retained the "field-proved advantages of the multi-function Custom Powr-Trol hydraulic system that provides effortless control of all types of equipment . . . Universal 3-Point Hitch with exclusive Load-and-Depth Control that makes 'pick up and go' farming more practical than ever . . . Advanced Power Steering that takes the muscle work out of driving the tractor . . . Independent Power Takeoff that enables you to handle PTO equipment more efficiently in heavy crops . . . the Float-Ride Seat that offers a gentle, floating ride in the roughest fields . . . Roll-O-Matic 'knee action' front wheels, now available in regular and heavy-duty types . . . Power-Adjusted Rear Wheels . . . quick-change front-end assemblies and many other features.

"Best of all, the performance that enabled John Deere tractors to set five fuel-economy records in official tests is yours in these new models. The exclusive 2-cylinder engine design that over the years has provided an enviable reputation for dependable, low-cost service will pave your way to greater profits. These tractors are available with a choice of engines—gasoline, LP-gas, all-fuel, and in the 730 Series you can choose the same diesel engine which set the all-time tractor fuel economy record," concluded the advertising. (The 830 was available only with a diesel engine.)

Photographed against lush modern-day corn with the sun setting over its shoulder, the 435 on the left represents the last 2-cylinder model of John Deere tractors introduced. Below: This 430 Standard Tractor is disking between closely spaced rows of New York grapes. Right: Increasingly more-comfortable seats and more-useful hydraulics evolved throughout the four-decade lifetime of John Deere 2-cylinder tractors.

Pages 148-149: This family portrait shows, in elegantly restored condition, an example of each of the six 30 Series models introduced in 1958. From left to right, the 1-2 plow 330 Standard . . . 2-3 plow 430 Tricycle . . . 3-plow General Purpose 530 . . . 4-plow 630 Standard (LP-gas) . . . 5-plow General Purpose 730 . . . and 6-plow 830 Standard. Like many of the other restored tractors pictured in this book, this photograph was taken in July 1987 at the site of the first Antique John Deere Tractor Expo near the municipal airport at Waterloo, Iowa.

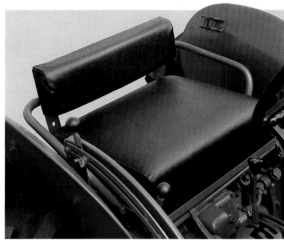

THE 'YELLOW' TRACTORS

Almost as soon as there were green John Deere tractors, there were "yellow" John Deere tractors; or at least, John Deere tractors modified for non-farm, industrial work.

The roots of today's John Deere Industrial Equipment can be traced back to the Waterloo Boy Tractor which was used in the early 1920s to pull graders over Iowa country roads. The Model "D" Tractor was occasionally painted "highway yellow" for road maintenance and other industrial applications. There were industrial options available for the "D" as early as 1925. However, the "DI" model designation didn't come along until 1935; the "AI" and "BI" in 1936. The Model "BI" was the most popular of the early John Deere industrial tractors. It was basically a modified Model "BR." The front casting was machined for attaching various types of industrial equipment: Vee plow, snow plow, push plate, rotary broom, loader and water pump. The rear axle bearings and shafts were made heavier to withstand bigger loads. The front axle was moved toward the rear to provide a shorter turning radius

and make possible closer coupling of attachments. The drawbar also was shortened and strengthened.

There also were "DIs," "AIs," "LIs," and "MIs" in the letter-series tractors, each modified in some way for non-farm industrial work. But the early crawler tractors may have the most legitimate ancestral claim on today's John Deere Industrial Equipment. In the early 1930s, there were two different types of Model "D" Crawler conversions. The Waterloo factory approach retained the conventional front-wheel steering and replaced the rear drive wheels with two-roller track-type treads. The other approach was the Lindeman crawler attachment which replaced the front and rear wheels and used the tracks for steering. The latter conversion evidently proved the most practical, because Lindeman subsequently developed crawler conversions for the orchard versions of the "GP" and "B" Tractors. The "BO" crawler proved to be the more popular.

In 1946, John Deere bought the Lindeman Manufacturing Company and continued to build crawler undercarriages in Yakima, Washington. In 1949, the Yakima Works developed a tool carrier and front

blade to mount on the small John Deere crawlers, converting them to bulldozers. In 1954, the Yakima Works was closed and production of crawlers and components was concentrated at the John Deere Dubuque (Iowa) Works where the Model "M" Tractors were manufactured.

Succeeding developments came fast: first, the 2-cylinder "MC" Crawler, then the 40C, followed by the 420 and the 430. Next came the 440. It was available with either a 2-cylinder John Deere engine or a 4-cylinder GMC diesel engine.

In 1959, the Waterloo factory built the 830I Tractor and the 840I Tractor primarily for use with a Hancock Scraper. Both the 830I and 840I had a 2-cylinder engine. These two units can be found even today on construction sites, moving soil and pulling compactors . . . a real tribute to the durability of the 2-cylinder engine.

The photograph on page 150 was taken in 1921 in Moline, Illinois. The Model "N" Waterloo Boy Tractor is pulling a city-owned road scraper. Shown below is the Industrial Line for 1959: 14 different wheel or track products, each with a 2-cylinder engine.

The 420I Tractor, right, is "spotting" a F9F5 jet fighter at the Naval Air Reserve Station at Wold-Chamberlain Field in Minneapolis, Minnesota. The photograph was taken in 1957.

Below at right is a Hawkeye Motor Patrol road grader powered by a John Deere "D" Tractor with dual rear wheels. Reproduced immediately below is a page from a 420 Crawler sales folder, pointing out the sales features of the "clustered" instrument panel. This panel was positioned directly in front of the operator where it could be "read" easily and reached quickly.

On page 153 is an early Model "D" Tractor with industrial options. Note the hard-rubber tires on the steel wheels and the large spark arrester. This "D" Industrial Tractor is pulling a road scraper and was photographed near Lincoln, Nebraska, in 1926.

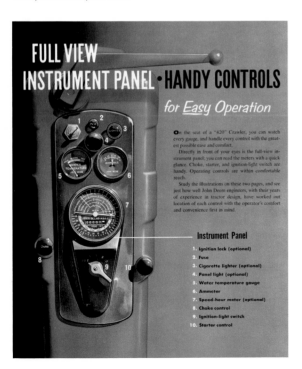

FULL VIEW INSTRUMENT PANEL · HANDY CONTROLS
for *Easy* Operation

On the seat of a "420" Crawler, you can watch every gauge, and handle every control with the greatest possible ease and comfort.

Directly in front of your eyes is the full-view instrument panel; you can read the meters with a quick glance. Choke, starter, and ignition-light switch are handy. Operating controls are within comfortable reach.

Study the illustrations on these two pages, and see just how well John Deere engineers, with their years of experience in tractor design, have worked out location of each control with the operator's comfort and convenience first in mind.

Instrument Panel

1. Ignition lock (optional)
2. Fuse
3. Cigarette lighter (optional)
4. Panel light (optional)
5. Water temperature gauge
6. Ammeter
7. Speed-hour meter (optional)
8. Choke control
9. Ignition-light switch
10. Starter control

Below is a styled Model "LI" Tractor with an integrally mounted 3-gang reel mower. It was photographed in 1939 on a golf course near Moline, Illinois.

The Model "BI" Tractor, below left, is pumping out a broken water main with a front-mounted centrifugal pump. Note that the pump is powered by the belt pulley.

The John Deere 40 Crawler at left is equipped with an outside-mounted bulldozer. It was photographed in 1952 near Moultrie, Georgia.

On page 154 is an "MI" Industrial Wheel Tractor painted "Nebraska Highway Orange." This tractor was painted John Deere green when the owner bought it for restoring. As he cleaned and took it apart, he discovered the original orange paint.

At right is the predecessor of today's John Deere industrial backhoe loader. It is a 1952 40 Utility Tractor with a Henry Loader and Pippin Backhoe. The 420 Crawler, below right, is equipped with an Ateco Loader. This photograph was taken in 1956.

"Pilot Touch" single stick control (below) was a sales feature of the early 440 Crawler. It gave the operator complete directional control—when it worked.

On page 157 are nine 320 Tractors, each equipped with a 7-foot sicklebar mower. This "fleet" was purchased in 1957 by the State Highway Department, Fort Worth, Texas.

JOHN DEERE
DOES IT AGAIN!

the

FIRST

SINGLE-
STICK
CONTROL

FOR CRAWLER

TRACTORS

In the late 1950s, the John Deere Waterloo Works built large industrial power units with 2-cylinder engines, having displacements of 471.5 cubic inches. The 840 diesel, below, with the "piggyback" Hancock Scraper, weighed 23,000 pounds. A beautifully restored 830I is shown at bottom left. The two industrial units at bottom right are 820Is. One has a "piggyback" scraper, the other is pulling a 4-wheel scraper.

On the next page are two 830Is. The front unit is pulling a pneumatic-wheel compactor and the rear unit is pulling a sheepsfoot compactor. This photograph was taken in 1959 near San Antonio, Texas.

resent and Past is the title of this Walter Haskell Hinton painting spanning the generations from the ox-drawn single-furrow plow to the four-furrow plow behind the "D." Not only the grandfather-father-son relationship, but also the John Deere tractor and plow symbolize the stability of rural life.

Artist Hinton was a master at painting people and animals in all types of action. When drawing and painting, Hinton worked from memory—with a minimum of reference photographs. Given a general description, he had the extraordinary ability to illustrate the given situation with incredible speed and accuracy. He also painted the illustrations reproduced on pages 1 and 56 of this book.

Authors: Donald S. Huber and Ralph C. Hughes. **Book Design:** Thomas A. Sizemore. **Photography:** John R. Boehm, Jack D. Cherry, Ralph C. Hughes, Thomas A. Sizemore, Rand L. Tapscott, Larry G. Volbruck, and Deere & Company Archives. **Research:** Special thanks to Leslie J. Stegh, Deere & Company Archivist and Jack D. Cherry, Two-Cylinder Club, for their help, guidance and suggestions.